JUMBLE®

Fiesta

A Celebration of Jumbling® Fun

Henri Arnold, Bob Lee, and Mike Argirion

TRIUMPH
BOOKS
CHICAGO

This book is available in quantity at special discounts
for your group or organization.

For further information, contact:

Triumph Books
814 North Franklin Street
Chicago, Illinois 60610

Printed in the United States of America

ISBN 978-1-57243-626-8

CONTENTS

JUMBLE®

Fiesta

Classic Puzzles

JUMBLE®

Unscramble these four Jumbles, one letter to each
square, to form four ordinary words.

WHISS

LOOGI

GRAHAN

HERTIE

WHAT THE GUARD
AT THE HAUNTED
HOUSE SAID.

Answer: ☐☐☐ ☐☐☐☐☐ THERE ?

JUMBLE®

Unscramble these four Jumbles, one letter to each square, to form four ordinary words.

LUSKK

GYLUL

BROJEB

GEAVAS

WHAT THOSE ANTS AT THE PICNIC DO.

Print answer here:

JUMBLE®

Unscramble these four Jumbles, one letter to each square, to form four ordinary words.

CAMKS

ZYCAR

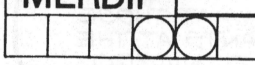

MERDIP

LOONED

WHAT HAPPENED WHEN HE ACCIDENTLY PULLED THE ALTITUDE STICK?

Answer: IT ⬡⬡⬡⬡ HIM " ⬡⬡⬡⬡ "

JUMBLE®

Unscramble these four Jumbles, one letter to each
square, to form four ordinary words.

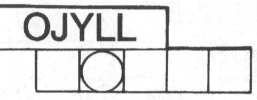

OJYLL

FAHFC

CEEDDO

SPELTE

Ha ha—but they
didn't get this

WHAT THE GUY WHO
HID HIS WALLET IN
THE FREEZER WAS
LEFT WITH.

Print answer here: ◯◯◯◯◯ ◯◯◯◯◯

5

JUMBLE®

Unscramble these four Jumbles, one letter to each square, to form four ordinary words.

HOVUC
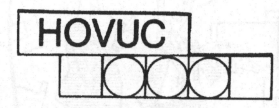

DINEK

RICCAT

FONTEM

BETTER NOT MAKE THIS KIND OF HOMEMADE BREAD.

Answer:

6

JUMBLE®

Unscramble these four Jumbles, one letter to each square, to form four ordinary words.

UPDYM

CRANF

CHROID

YAUBET

Get me out! Get me out!

He's supposed to be quite a swinger

WHAT THE GUY WHO GOT STUCK IN A REVOLVING DOOR DOESN'T GET ANYMORE.

Answer here: ◯◯◯◯◯◯ ◯◯◯◯◯

JUMBLE®

Unscramble these four Jumbles, one letter to each square, to form four ordinary words.

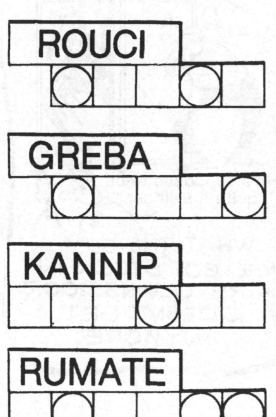

ROUCI

GREBA

KANNIP

RUMATE

Glad to make your acquaintance

WHAT SOME SKATERS MIGHT HAVE TO DO IN ORDER TO GET BETTER ACQUAINTED.

Print answer here: ◯◯◯◯◯ THE ◯◯◯

JUMBLE®

Unscramble these four Jumbles, one letter to each
square, to form four ordinary words.

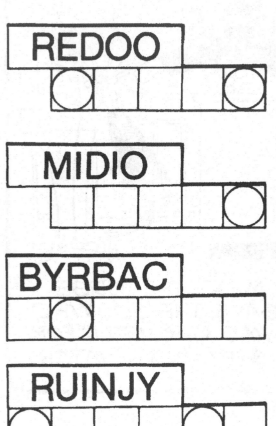

REDOO

MIDIO

BYRBAC

RUINJY

HE DECIDED TO
WATCH HIS DRINKING—
BY ONLY VISITING BARS
THAT HAVE THIS.

Print answer here: A

JUMBLE®

Unscramble these four Jumbles, one letter to each square, to form four ordinary words.

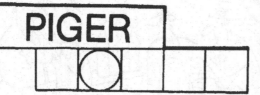

PIGER

SEPOI

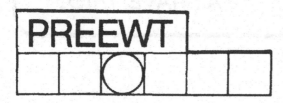

KAJLAC

PREEWT

WHAT THE JUDGE GAVE THE GUY WHO WAS ARRESTED FOR STEALING A WATCH.

Print answer here: THE ""

JUMBLE®

Unscramble these four Jumbles, one letter to each square, to form four ordinary words.

RALNS

MARDA

CASSEC

VAHDLE

Let's take a rest

WHAT THE GUY WHO WAS "ALL FEET" WHEN HE DANCED WAS WHEN THEY SAT DOWN.

Print answer here: ☐☐☐ ☐☐☐☐☐

JUMBLE®

Unscramble these four Jumbles, one letter to each square, to form four ordinary words.

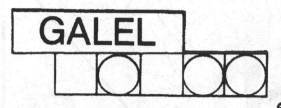

GALEL

HOTBO

FRAIDT

WARROM

WHAT THE BLIND DATE SHE WAS LOOKING FORWARD TO MEETING TURNED OUT TO BE.

Answer: A " ⬚⬚⬚⬚⬚ ⬚⬚⬚⬚⬚ "

JUMBLE®

Unscramble these four Jumbles, one letter to each square, to form four ordinary words.

YEHRM

DAUTI

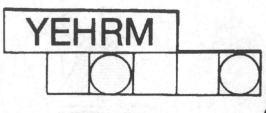

PHARME

RYNFEZ

CLANG CLANG

IF SHE EVER TOLD HER REAL AGE, HER BIRTHDAY CAKE WOULD BE THIS.

Answer here: A ⬡⬡⬡⬡ ⬡⬡⬡⬡⬡⬡

JUMBLE®

Unscramble these four Jumbles, one letter to each square, to form four ordinary words.

NARPO

HAWRT

TELSED

PRULAB

IN ORDER TO FIND OUT WHICH KIND OF ICE-CREAM SODA IS THE BEST, TAKE THIS.

Answer: A " ⬡⬡⬡⬡⬡⬡ " ⬡⬡⬡⬡

JUMBLE®

Unscramble these four Jumbles, one letter to each square, to form four ordinary words.

GHUDO

VELGO

BLOMIE

MECION

Hi, sweetie

NEEDED TO IMPRESS A LAUNDRESS.

Print answer here: A ☐☐☐☐ ☐☐☐☐

JUMBLE®

Unscramble these four Jumbles, one letter to each
square, to form four ordinary words.

MIRPE

ZYIZD

BREPUS

PREJUM

> But, PLEASE, dear. . .
> let me explain. . .

> WHAT HE OFTEN
> DID BEHIND
> HIS WIFE'S BACK.

Answer here: ◯◯◯◯◯◯ HER ◯◯

JUMBLE®

Unscramble these four Jumbles, one letter to each square, to form four ordinary words.

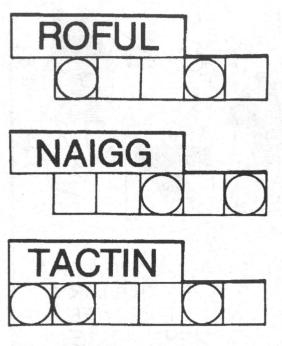

ROFUL

NAIGG

TACTIN

GERELD

HER FACE IS HER FORTUNE, AND IT RUNS INTO THIS.

Answer here: A ◯◯◯◯ ◯◯◯◯◯◯

JUMBLE®

Unscramble these four Jumbles, one letter to each
square, to form four ordinary words.

AVERB

NEYOH

NOAWHY

DEGULC

HE HAD A "PEACH"
OF A SECRETARY
UNTIL HIS WIFE
ORDERED THIS.

Answer here: ⬡⬡⬡ " ⬡⬡⬡⬡⬡⬡ "

JUMBLE®

Unscramble these four Jumbles, one letter to each
square, to form four ordinary words.

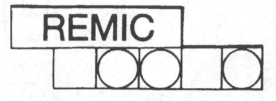

REMIC
⬜🔘🔘⬜🔘

SELIA
⬜🔘🔘🔘⬜

ACCUST
🔘⬜🔘🔘⬜⬜

TONKYT
🔘⬜⬜⬜⬜🔘

Guess I'd better
bundle up

COULD IT BE A
RAINCOAT FOR WEAR
IN THE BIGTOWN?

Answer: A ⬜🔘🔘🔘🔘 🔘🔘🔘🔘🔘🔘🔘

JUMBLE®

Unscramble these four Jumbles, one letter to each square, to form four ordinary words.

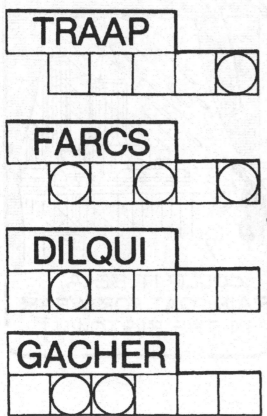

TRAAP

FARCS

DILQUI

GACHER

SOME PEOPLE KEEP
TRYING ON SHOES
UNTIL THE SALESMAN
DOES THIS.

Print answer here:

JUMBLE.

Unscramble these four Jumbles, one letter to each square, to form four ordinary words.

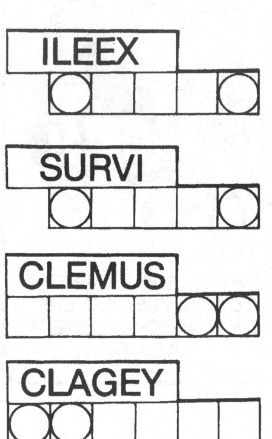

ILEEX

SURVI

CLEMUS

CLAGEY

HOW FAR DOWN WAS HER BATHING SUIT CUT?

Answer here: TO " ◯◯◯ " ◯◯◯◯◯◯

JUMBLE®

Unscramble these four Jumbles, one letter to each square, to form four ordinary words.

PROOD

HIWEL

SLINUM

DRATOW

WHY THE BUSINESS TYCOON RUSHED OFF ON A MUCH NEEDED VACATION.

Print answer here: TO

JUMBLE®

Unscramble these four Jumbles, one letter to each square, to form four ordinary words.

CIHRB

LUCOT

NOYFLE

INDIGH

I demand that my client continue to be supported in the manner to which she has been accustomed

WHY HIS EX-WIFE TOOK HIM TO THE CLEANERS.

Answer: HE WAS

JUMBLE®

Unscramble these four Jumbles, one letter to each square, to form four ordinary words.

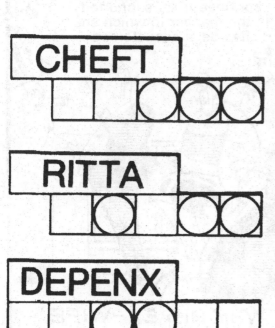

CHEFT

RITTA

DEPENX

YURKET

WHAT HE AND HIS GIRL WERE.

Answer:  ◯◯◯◯◯◯ ◯◯◯◯◯

JUMBLE

Unscramble these four Jumbles, one letter to each square, to form four ordinary words.

GITUL

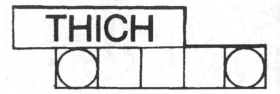

THICH

GROUME

METHEL

Sick friend...

WHAT THE INVISIBLE MAN'S WIFE SAW WHEN HER HUSBAND GAVE HIS USUAL LAME EXCUSE.

Answer: RIGHT ◯◯◯◯◯◯◯ ◯◯◯

JUMBLE®

Unscramble these four Jumbles, one letter to each square, to form four ordinary words.

ORRGI

GUNDE

NELPOY

FLUTAR

THEY RESENTED THAT RITZY POOCH BECAUSE HE ALWAYS WANTED TO DO THIS.

Print answer here: ◯◯◯ ON THE ◯◯◯

26

JUMBLE®

Fiesta

Daily Puzzles

PUZZLE
26

JUMBLE®

Unscramble these four Jumbles, one letter to each
square, to form four ordinary words.

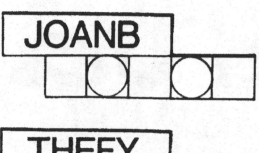

JOANB

THEFY

CALKAJ

SLIZZE

WHAT A COWARD
MIGHT DO
WHEN HE GETS
INTO A "JAM."

Answer:  LIKE

28

JUMBLE®

Unscramble these four Jumbles, one letter to each square, to form four ordinary words.

TEFIB

WOGIN

YORPTS

DARCCO

He never likes the pieces we're doing

REGARDLESS OF WHAT THE ORCHESTRA PERFORMS, THE BASS PLAYER HAS TO DO THIS.

Print answer here: ◯◯◯◯◯◯ ◯◯◯ IT

JUMBLE®

Unscramble these four Jumbles, one letter to each
square, to form four ordinary words.

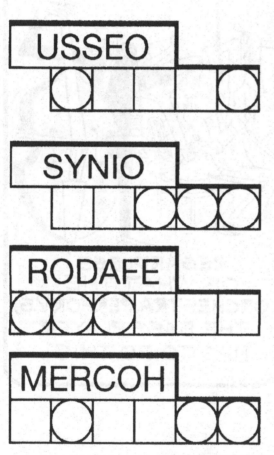

USSEO

SYNIO

RODAFE

MERCOH

Just practicing our
casts, officer

RESTRICTED
AREA

WHY THE GAME
WARDEN DIDN'T
BELIEVE HIS
STORY.

Answer here : IT ⬡⬡⬡⬡⬡⬡ ⬡⬡⬡⬡⬡

JUMBLE®

Unscramble these four Jumbles, one letter to each square, to form four ordinary words.

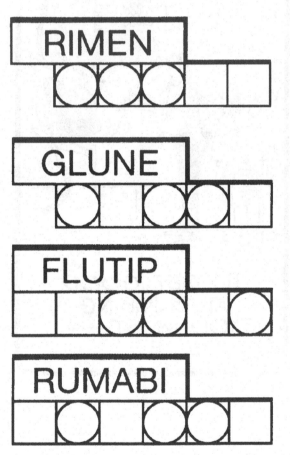

RIMEN

GLUNE

FLUTIP

RUMABI

Watch your shadows

WHAT THE YOUNG PHOTOGRAPHER THOUGHT THE LIGHTING LESSON WAS.

Answer :

JUMBLE®

Unscramble these four Jumbles, one letter to each
square, to form four ordinary words.

ARBSS

RUHYR

LESPEN

TIPOLE

That's your fastest time

He practices
10 times
a day

TO GET GOOD
AT CLIMBING
YOU MUST----

Answer here : ◯◯◯◯◯ THE ◯◯◯◯◯

32

JUMBLE®

Unscramble these four Jumbles, one letter to each square, to form four ordinary words.

KYMOS

GEGAU

ANFLOG

YIPRAC

CLASS OF '86

I guess this is what we've been looking forward to

WHAT GRADUATION TIME WAS FOR THOSE YOUNG PEOPLE.

Answer here: THE " ⬡⬡⬡⬡ " OF ⬡⬡⬡⬡

JUMBLE®

Unscramble these four Jumbles, one letter to each square, to form four ordinary words.

VEDEL
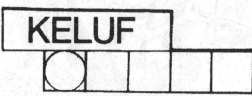

KELUF
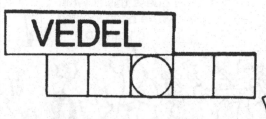

RAMAAD

LAPLID
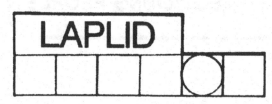

I remember it as though it were yesterday

WHAT A PHOTO-GRAPHIC MEMORY NEVER SEEMS TO RUN OUT OF.

Print answer here:

JUMBLE

Unscramble these four Jumbles, one letter to each square, to form four ordinary words.

GYROL

GURAU

FLENNE

CHISPY

Not much upstairs

But she can sure dance

WHAT A DANCER'S REPUTATION OFTEN RESTS UPON.

Print answer here:

35

JUMBLE®

Unscramble these four Jumbles, one letter to each square, to form four ordinary words.

UGLIE

SNAIB

FRODIL

TEXCIE

SPECIALS TODAY:
Fried snakes
Broiled eels
Baked octopus

FOOD SOME PEOPLE
FIND EDIBLE
MIGHT SEEM
THIS TO OTHERS.

Print answer here:

JUMBLE®

Unscramble these four Jumbles, one letter to each
square, to form four ordinary words.

ROCKA

SEDUE

RYPTAN

BOTHED

HOW AN
OSTEOPATH WORKS
HIS FINGERS.

Answer here: TO ⬡⬡⬡⬡⬡ ⬡⬡⬡⬡⬡

JUMBLE®

Unscramble these four Jumbles, one letter to each
square, to form four ordinary words.

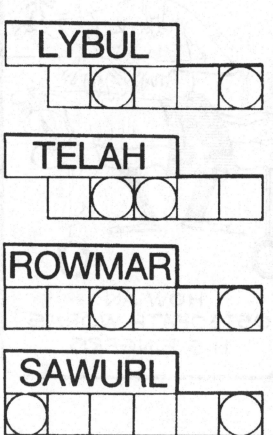

LYBUL

TELAH

ROWMAR

SAWURL

Move it! How can I beat
the competition?!

HOW THE
SAUSAGE MANU-
FACTURER WANTED
TO MAKE MONEY.

Answer here: IN THE " ◯◯◯◯◯◯ " ◯◯◯

38

JUMBLE®

Unscramble these four Jumbles, one letter to each
square, to form four ordinary words.

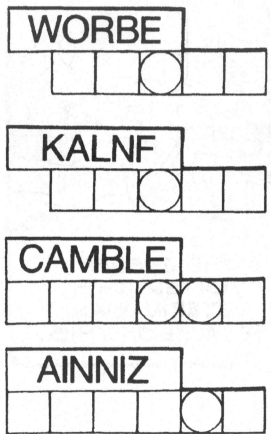

WORBE

KALNF

CAMBLE

AINNIZ

WHERE THERE'S A
WILL THERE'S
SOMETIMES THIS.

Print answer here:

JUMBLE®

Unscramble these four Jumbles, one letter to each
square, to form four ordinary words.

CANEP

PLIMB

ONBEAM

VINOSI

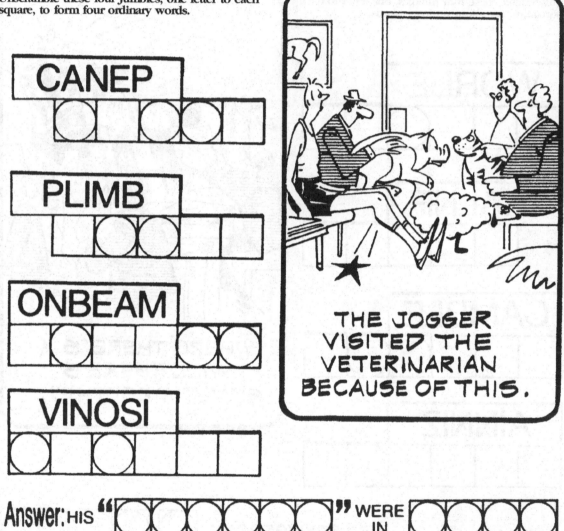

THE JOGGER
VISITED THE
VETERINARIAN
BECAUSE OF THIS.

Answer: HIS " ☐☐☐☐☐☐ " WERE ☐☐☐☐
IN

JUMBLE®

Unscramble these four Jumbles, one letter to each square, to form four ordinary words.

VOPER

RODLE

SHAUTI

DEECES

He sure gets results

WHAT A GOOD
SALESMAN KNOWS
HOW TO BRING.

Answer: ☐☐☐☐☐☐ OUT OF ☐☐☐☐☐☐

41

JUMBLE®

Unscramble these four Jumbles, one letter to each square, to form four ordinary words.

MIRGY

NAHCT

WOLTAL

VEWERS

Sorry I won't be able to make our anniversary party, dear

PEOPLE WHO ARE TOO ANXIOUS TO MAKE A LIVING HAVE SOMETIMES FORGOTTEN THIS.

Print answer here: ◯◯◯ TO ◯◯◯◯◯

JUMBLE®

Unscramble these four Jumbles, one letter to each square, to form four ordinary words.

MYTIA

DENUC

CULIES

RUMMRU

WHAT THE
ORGAN GRINDER
HAD.

Answer: A " ⬡⬡⬡⬡ " FOR ⬡⬡⬡⬡⬡

JUMBLE®

Unscramble these four Jumbles, one letter to each
square, to form four ordinary words.

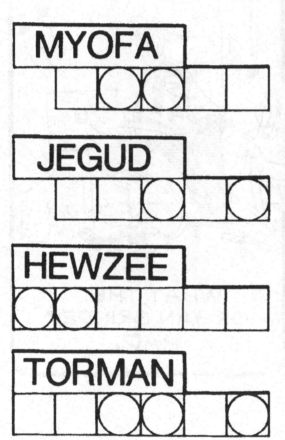

MYOFA

JEGUD

HEWZEE

TORMAN

Wait'll they see the results
of these exams!

WHERE THE
GEOLOGY PRO-
FESSOR BROUGHT
HIS STUDENTS.

Answer here: ⬡⬡⬡⬡ TO ⬡⬡⬡⬡⬡

JUMBLE®

Unscramble these four Jumbles, one letter to each square, to form four ordinary words.

DIPAL

MESOU

GNININ

VARSOY

Fifty years from now, you'll ...

WHAT AN OPTOMETRIST IS.

Answer here: A ⬡⬡⬡ OF ⬡⬡⬡⬡⬡⬡

JUMBLE®

Unscramble these four Jumbles, one letter to each square, to form four ordinary words.

GRITE

OMENG

STEEWF

HISBUL

EVERY TIME
BABY CRIED THEY
GAVE HIM THIS.

Answer: THE " ◯◯◯◯◯ " ◯◯◯◯◯◯

JUMBLE®

Unscramble these four Jumbles, one letter to each
square, to form four ordinary words.

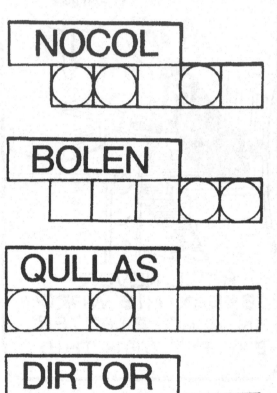

NOCOL

BOLEN

QULLAS

DIRTOR

A WOMAN GOES TO A
HAIR STYLIST WHEN
SHE DOESN'T WANT
TO SHOW THIS.

Answer: HER ☐☐☐☐☐ ☐☐☐☐☐☐☐

JUMBLE

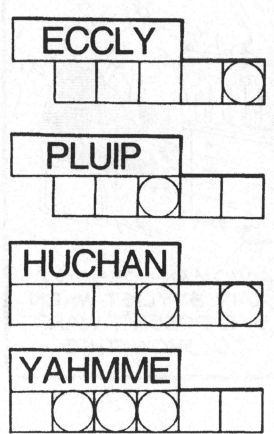

Unscramble these four Jumbles, one letter to each square, to form four ordinary words.

ECCLY

PLUIP

HUCHAN

YAHMME

Forever and ever...

HE'LL NEVER BREAK HIS WORD IN A LOVE LETTER, EXCEPT WITH THIS.

Print answer here:

JUMBLE®

Unscramble these four Jumbles, one letter to each
square, to form four ordinary words.

HIWGE

LOFUR

BRONIN

DELBEH

HE PICKED A SOFT
JOB BECAUSE
HE EXPECTED
TO DO THIS LATER.

Print answer here: ⃝⃝⃝ ⃝⃝⃝⃝ ON
IT

JUMBLE®

Unscramble these four Jumbles, one letter to each square, to form four ordinary words.

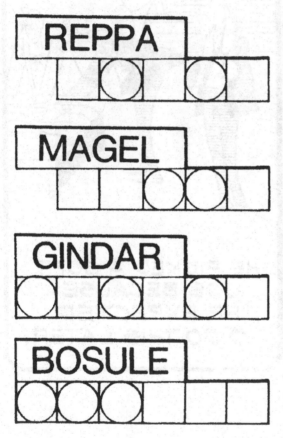

REPPA

MAGEL

GINDAR

BOSULE

His work has made him rich

HOW A PASTRY CHEF DOESN'T LIVE.

Answer here: BY ◯◯◯◯◯◯ ◯◯◯◯◯

JUMBLE

Unscramble these four Jumbles, one letter to each
square, to form four ordinary words.

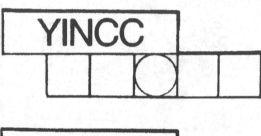

YINCC

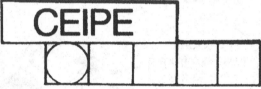

CEIPE

FITTOU

BLOMAG

WHAT SORT OF
JOB DO THEY DO
DELIVERING
PARCELS?

Print answer here: A " ⬡⬡⬡⬡⬡ – ⬡⬡ " ONE

JUMBLE®

Unscramble these four Jumbles, one letter to each square, to form four ordinary words.

HIMEC

MESOO

BEEDAT

TRUXAS

I wouldn't trust him from here to the door

WHAT A POLITICIAN'S LIFE OFTEN IS.

Answer here: A ◯◯◯ OF "◯◯◯◯◯"

JUMBLE®

Unscramble these four Jumbles, one letter to each square, to form four ordinary words.

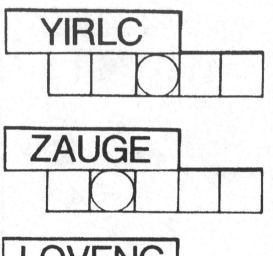

YIRLC

ZAUGE

LOVENC

GAFINC

You devil, you!

WHAT YOU WILL NEVER HAVE IF YOU FALL IN LOVE WITH YOURSELF.

Print answer here:

JUMBLE®

Unscramble these four Jumbles, one letter to each square, to form four ordinary words.

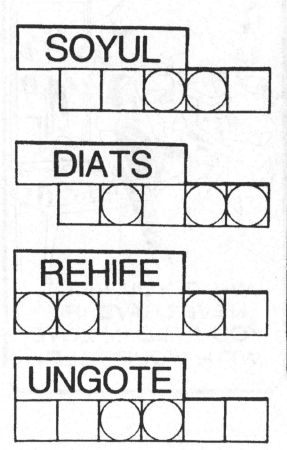

SOYUL

DIATS

REHIFE

UNGOTE

IN GERMANY, IT MIGHT PROVIDE THE ANSWER TO THE COMMON COLD.

Answer here: "◯◯◯◯◯◯◯◯◯◯◯◯◯"

JUMBLE®

Unscramble these four Jumbles, one letter to each square, to form four ordinary words.

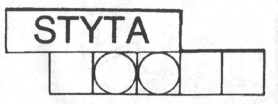

STYTA

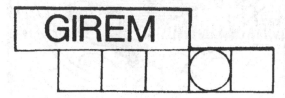

GIREM

ENKASH

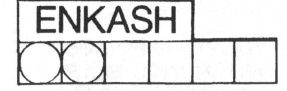

IROING

HOW A WAR-MONGER BELIEVES IN TALKING.

Print answer here: WITH

JUMBLE®

Unscramble these four Jumbles, one letter to each square, to form four ordinary words.

TYTUN

HELEW

LEEMOT

NOBBOA

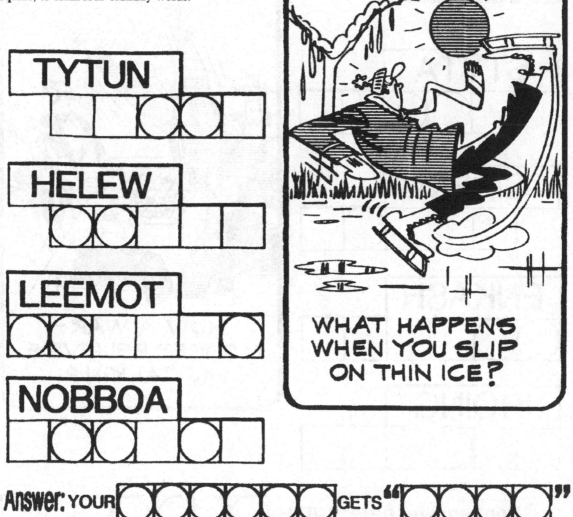

WHAT HAPPENS WHEN YOU SLIP ON THIN ICE?

Answer: YOUR ⬡⬡⬡⬡⬡⬡ GETS "⬡⬡⬡⬡"

PUZZLE

55

JUMBLE®

Unscramble these four Jumbles, one letter to each square, to form four ordinary words.

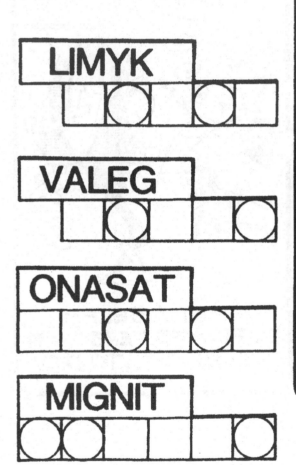

LIMYK

VALEG

ONASAT

MIGNIT

HE HAD THE SELF-CONTROL TO GIVE UP DRINKING AND SMOKING BUT NOT THE SELF-CONTROL TO GIVE UP THIS.

Answer here: ☐☐☐☐☐☐☐ ABOUT ☐☐

JUMBLE®

Unscramble these four Jumbles, one letter to each square, to form four ordinary words.

OUDES

TOIDI

SABBOR

KLEESH

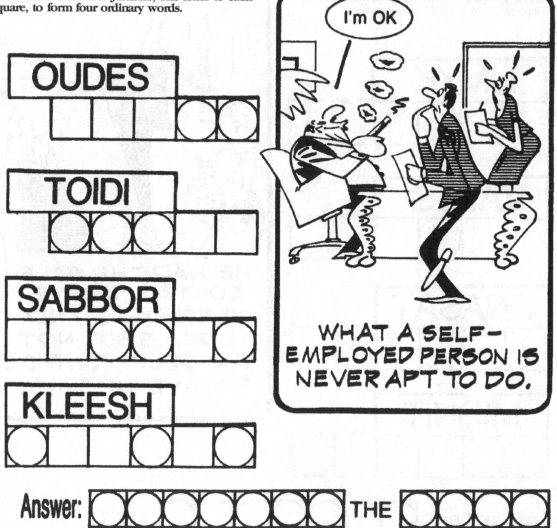

I'm OK

WHAT A SELF—
EMPLOYED PERSON IS
NEVER APT TO DO.

Answer: [ ] [ ] [ ] [ ] [ ] [ ] THE [ ] [ ] [ ] [ ]

JUMBLE®

Unscramble these four Jumbles, one letter to each square, to form four ordinary words.

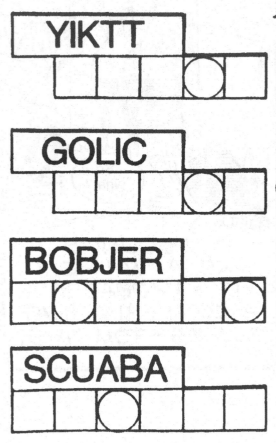

YIKTT

GOLIC

BOBJER

SCUABA

WHAT TWO WRONGS SOMETIMES ACTUALLY DO MAKE.

Print answer here: ◯ " ◯◯◯◯ "

JUMBLE®

Unscramble these four Jumbles, one letter to each square, to form four ordinary words.

SUMIN

COSUR

GOYAVE

RUPPLE

They won the lottery!

So what?

IF IT SOUNDS LIKE A "WHINE," IT'S PROBABLY A COMPLAINT THAT COMES FROM THIS.

Answer here:

JUMBLE

Unscramble these four Jumbles, one letter to each square, to form four ordinary words.

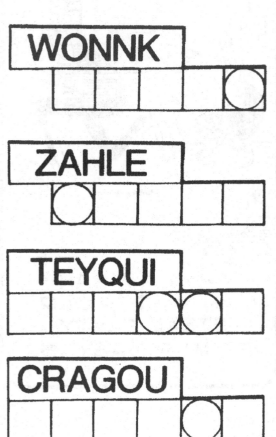

WONNK

ZAHLE

TEYQUI

CRAGOU

Why not also take my house and car?

THAT NEXT-DOOR NEIGHBOR WHO'S ALWAYS BORROWING YOUR STUFF WILL TAKE ANYTHING FROM YOU EXCEPT THIS.

Print answer here:

JUMBLE®

Unscramble these four Jumbles, one letter to each
square, to form four ordinary words.

GUGOE

ULIQT

DOYLEM

HESTEE

WHAT A MEAN
MAN WHO WOULD
STEAL CANDY
FROM A BABY IS.

Answer: A [◯◯◯◯] WITHOUT " [◯◯◯◯] "
A

JUMBLE®

Unscramble these four Jumbles, one letter to each square, to form four ordinary words.

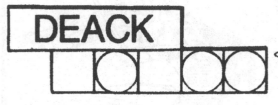

DEACK

LEREB

RENARB

ONSWID

Lovely day

Yeah, but for tomorrow rain is forecast

A PESSIMIST IS ALWAYS GOOD FOR THIS.

Print answer here:

PUZZLE
62

JUMBLE®

Unscramble these four Jumbles, one letter to each
square, to form four ordinary words.

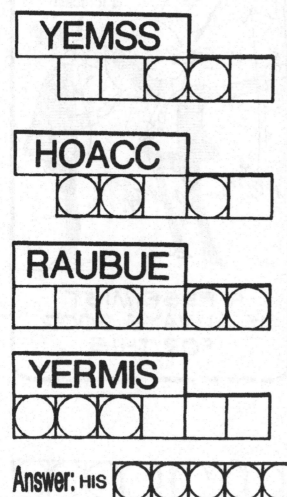

YEMSS

HOACC

RAUBUE

YERMIS

WHAT THE BRIDGE
ON THE VIOLIN
ENABLES THE
PLAYER TO GET.

Answer: HIS ⬡⬡⬡⬡⬡ "⬡⬡⬡⬡⬡⬡"

PUZZLE 63

JUMBLE®

Unscramble these four Jumbles, one letter to each square, to form four ordinary words.

GINTY

CNOTH

MUSSIE

SAVILE

WHAT THE BOY SNAKE SAID TO THE GIRL SNAKE.

Answer here: ⬡⬡⬡⬡ US A ⬡⬡⬡⬡

JUMBLE®

Unscramble these four Jumbles, one letter to each square, to form four ordinary words.

UGLLY

NIRAY

NOBARC

TEPROY

Charge!

NAPOLEON WAS THE FIRST MAN WHO THOUGHT HE WAS THIS.

Print answer here:

JUMBLE®

Unscramble these four Jumbles, one letter to each square, to form four ordinary words.

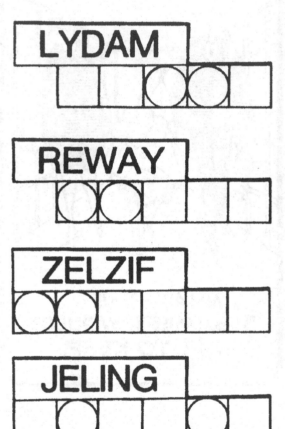

LYDAM

REWAY

ZELZIF

JELING

FORMERLY FOUND ONLY IN THE COUNTRY BUT NOW COMMONLY SEEN IN THE CITY.

Print answer here:

JUMBLE®

Unscramble these four Jumbles, one letter to each square, to form four ordinary words.

TALNS

MANUH

INLOVI

FLUWOE

He won't talk to anyone

WHAT THE BIGAMIST WOULD LIKE TO KEEP.

Answer here: " ◯◯◯ " ◯◯◯◯◯◯◯◯

JUMBLE®

Unscramble these four Jumbles, one letter to each
square, to form four ordinary words.

KAWOE

ROMIN

GEDDUR

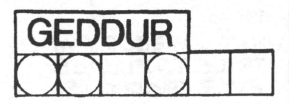

GEPPIN

See you around

ANOTHER NAME
FOR A
PHILANDERER.

Answer: A ◯◯◯◯◯ ◯◯◯◯◯◯◯◯

JUMBLE®

Unscramble these four Jumbles, one letter to each square, to form four ordinary words.

NUDOM

BOGUM

NUMOTT

EBONGY

You're always _____ right, J.B.!

WHAT SOMEBODY WHO TRIES TO PLEASE EVERYBODY IS APT TO REMAIN.

Print answer here: A

JUMBLE®

Unscramble these four Jumbles, one letter to each square, to form four ordinary words.

FILOO

IVGLI

BONBBI

GURCOH

WHAT WERE
ALEXANDER
GRAHAM BELL'S
FIRST WORDS?

Print answer here:

JUMBLE®

Unscramble these four Jumbles, one letter to each square, to form four ordinary words.

GEWED

NARBD

YIKELL

REWEPT

Can't find a thing wrong with you

You're not trying!

WHAT THE HYPOCHONDRIAC WAS SICK OF.

Print answer here: ⬡⬡⬡⬡⬡⬡ ⬡⬡⬡⬡

JUMBLE®

Unscramble these four Jumbles, one letter to each square, to form four ordinary words.

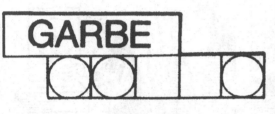

GARBE

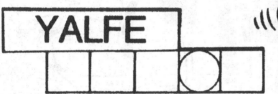

YALFE

NATTYR

HOLURY

WHAT THEY CALLED HER HUSBAND WHO WAS ADDICTED TO GAMBLING.

Answer: HER " ⃞⃞⃞⃞⃞⃞⃞ " ⃞⃞⃞⃞

JUMBLE®

Unscramble these four Jumbles, one letter to each square, to form four ordinary words.

FLECT

UGIED

KONYED

LANFEX

A DAY OFF IS SOMETIMES FOLLOWED BY THIS.

Print answer here: AN ◯◯◯ ◯◯◯

JUMBLE®

Unscramble these four Jumbles, one letter to each square, to form four ordinary words.

IXOCT

CATHY

GRUHNY

WURCEF

WHAT THAT ROAD HOG BELIEVES "MIGHT" MAKES.

Answer: ⬡⬡⬡⬡⬡ — ⬡⬡⬡⬡⬡

75

JUMBLE®

Unscramble these four Jumbles, one letter to each square, to form four ordinary words.

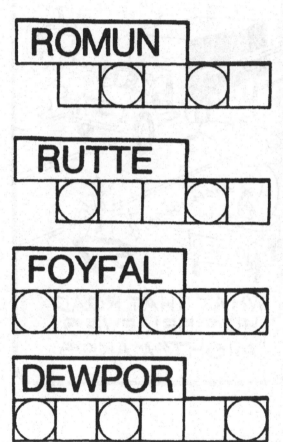

ROMUN

RUTTE

FOYFAL

DEWPOR

WHAT YEAST IS.

Answer here: ☐◯◯◯◯◯ ◯◯◯◯◯

JUMBLE®

Unscramble these four Jumbles, one letter to each square, to form four ordinary words.

VEELA

JOMAR

HOCCUR

BRUETT

WHAT THE OUTLAWS TURNED SKYDIVERS HAD.

Answer here: A "◯◯◯◯◯◯" ◯◯◯

JUMBLE®

Unscramble these four Jumbles, one letter to each
square, to form four ordinary words.

FROYE

NEARY

TESSMY

HERTAH

Don't bother me—you
shouldn't have bought
this pile of junk!

A PERSON WHO
ALWAYS BORROWS
TROUBLE IS
USUALLY ANXIOUS
TO DO THIS.

Answer: ⬡⬡⬡⬡⬡ IT WITH ⬡⬡⬡⬡⬡⬡⬡

JUMBLE®

Unscramble these four Jumbles, one letter to each
square, to form four ordinary words.

AGELL

TIARE

DARNBY

TARIBB

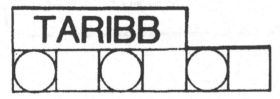

Now that we're so rich,
you'll have time to fix the
fence one of these days

ANOTHER NAME
FOR SARCASM.

Answer here: ⬡⬡⬡⬡⬡⬡ "⬡⬡⬡"

JUMBLE®

Unscramble these four Jumbles, one letter to each square, to form four ordinary words.

NOMEW

DOIMI

THOTEG

STOJEL

HE LIES IN WAIT
FOR A FISH,
AND AFTER CATCHING
IT HE DOES THIS.

Answer here: ⬡⬡⬡⬡ IN ⬡⬡⬡⬡⬡⬡

JUMBLE®

Unscramble these four Jumbles, one letter to each
square, to form four ordinary words.

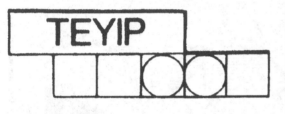
TEYIP

WARFE

FORLEG

VITHER

WHAT THE BUS
DRIVER TOLD HIM.

Answer:

TO

JUMBLE®

Unscramble these four Jumbles, one letter to each
square, to form four ordinary words.

BREYD

TOJUS

SAKMAD

NELPOL

I guess he has no
more time for me

A WOMAN CAN
SAY MORE IN
A LOOK THAN A
MAN CAN IN THIS.

Print answer here: ⬡ ⬡⬡⬡⬡

JUMBLE®

Unscramble these four Jumbles, one letter to each square, to form four ordinary words.

MYFIL

RECSS

GINOUT

HAWRTT

ON A BLIND DATE
HE WAS EXPECTING
A "VISION,"
BUT IT TURNED
OUT TO BE THIS.

Print answer here:

JUMBLE®

Unscramble these four Jumbles, one letter to each
square, to form four ordinary words.

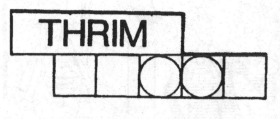

THRIM

CITHY

WURPAD

RASHEE

Every time he opens his
mouth he reveals
his ignorance

ONE WAY TO
SAVE FACE
IS TO LEARN
TO KEEP THIS.

Answer here:  OF IT

JUMBLE®

Unscramble these four Jumbles, one letter to each square, to form four ordinary words.

TIGAN

RAMOA

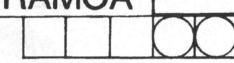
SHORUC

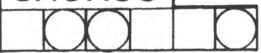
TULIED

I can't see myself getting rich here. Think I'll quit

IF A JOB IS TO HAVE A FUTURE, IT'S LIKELY TO DEPEND ON THIS.

Answer: THE  WHO

JUMBLE®

Unscramble these four Jumbles, one letter to each
square, to form four ordinary words.

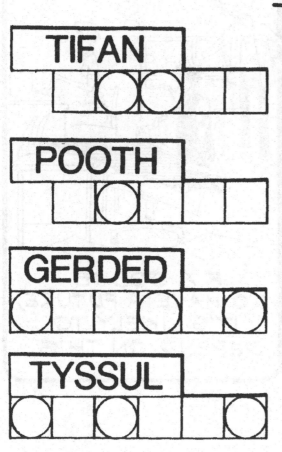

TIFAN

POOTH

GERDED

TYSSUL

A GUY WHO'S
ALWAYS BOASTING
ABOUT HIS FAMILY
TREE PROBABLY
COMES FROM THIS.

Answer here: ITS ⬡⬡⬡⬡⬡ ⬡⬡⬡⬡

JUMBLE®

Unscramble these four Jumbles, one letter to each square, to form four ordinary words.

MAFER

THICH

UNCOBE

BUESAD

Looks gorgeous on you!

SHE HAS WHAT IT TAKES TO WEAR THE LATEST FASHIONS——

Answer: A ⬡⬡⬡⬡⬡ ⬡⬡⬡⬡⬡⬡⬡⬡

JUMBLE®

Unscramble these four Jumbles, one letter to each
square, to form four ordinary words.

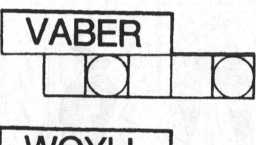

VABER

WOYLL

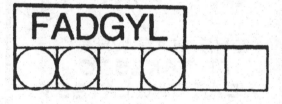

FADGYL

NURTHE

THAT WINDBAG
WAS ALWAYS GET-
TING CARRIED AWAY
BY THE SOUND
OF HIS OWN VOICE,
BUT NEVER THIS.

Print answer here:

JUMBLE®

Unscramble these four Jumbles, one letter to each square, to form four ordinary words.

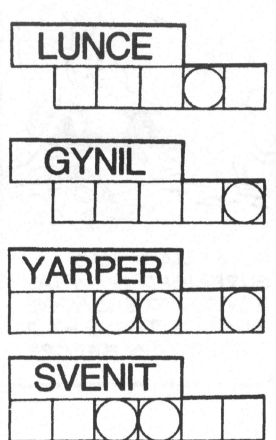

LUNCE

GYNIL

YARPER

SVENIT

HOW THE
UNDERTAKER
PRESENTED
HIS BILL.

Print answer here:

JUMBLE®

Unscramble these four Jumbles, one letter to each square, to form four ordinary words.

NEETA

FECEN

DRIHNE

INDATE

GOLIATH WAS SURPRISED BY WHAT DAVID DID BECAUSE SUCH A THING HAD NEVER THIS BEFORE.

Answer:  HIS

JUMBLE®

Unscramble these four Jumbles, one letter to each square, to form four ordinary words.

HOTOT

PECOU

LIKLER

LANDAV

SHE WAS NEVER OVERLOOKED, BUT USUALLY THIS.

Answer here:

JUMBLE®

Unscramble these four Jumbles, one letter to each square, to form four ordinary words.

KANOE

GREME

LASTOP

ENMURB

I knew it all along

A PERSON WHO WAKES UP TO FIND HIMSELF FAMOUS MAY NOT HAVE THIS.

Answer here:

JUMBLE®

Unscramble these four Jumbles, one letter to each square, to form four ordinary words.

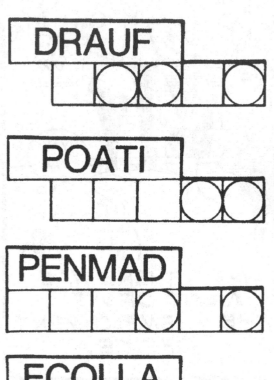

DRAUF

POATI

PENMAD

ECOLLA

How about a drink?

Just a wee one

THAT VISITOR WHO DROPS IN FOR A CALL MIGHT ACTUALLY BE WANTING TO DO THIS.

Answer: ⬭⬭⬭⬭ ⬭⬭ FOR A ⬭⬭⬭⬭

JUMBLE

Unscramble these four Jumbles, one letter to each square, to form four ordinary words.

RILLT

ZYZID

DAPNIK

SEATTL

A—E

YAK YAK

Next!

YAK YAK

WHAT THERE WAS A LOT OF AT THE UNEMPLOYMENT OFFICE.

Print answer here: " ⬡⬡⬡⬡ " ⬡⬡⬡⬡

JUMBLE®

Unscramble these four Jumbles, one letter to each
square, to form four ordinary words.

TCHAB

KORJE

DILQUI

UPVERY

WHEN THE KIDS
HAVE TO PLAY
IN ON ACCOUNT OF
BAD WEATHER,
THE PARENTS OFTEN
END UP THIS WAY.

Print answer here:

JUMBLE®

Unscramble these four Jumbles, one letter to each
square, to form four ordinary words.

ORPOD

VALAR

YURELS

PICHER

WHAT THE
INTELLECTUAL
HOBO WAS.

Answer: A

96

JUMBLE®

Unscramble these four Jumbles, one letter to each
square, to form four ordinary words.

AKQUE

DRATY

LESCUM

DAGAPO

A BLAZE
CAN BE VERY
HOT, ESPECIALLY
WHEN IT'S THIS.

Print answer here: " ⃝⃝⃝⃝⃝⃝ "

JUMBLE®

Unscramble these four Jumbles, one letter to each square, to form four ordinary words.

MUTOH

PARAT

GANDIL

THRENE

WHAT A WOMAN MIGHT ATTEMPT TO DRAW WITH AN EYEBROW PENCIL.

Print answer here:

JUMBLE

Unscramble these four Jumbles, one letter to each square, to form four ordinary words.

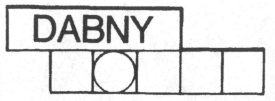

DABNY

OMPET

TUCLED

YERECH

Wait'll I get finished with him!

WHAT THE "HAM" WAS FOR THE DRAMA CRITIC.

Print answer here: HIS " ◯◯◯◯ "

JUMBLE®

Unscramble these four Jumbles, one letter to each square, to form four ordinary words.

Get lost!

A GIRL WHO NOW TELLS HIM WHERE TO TAKE HER MIGHT LATER TELL HIM THIS.

NOPLY

DUGEF

CHAWES

TRIEHD

Print answer here: ◯◯◯◯◯ TO ◯◯

JUMBLE®

Unscramble these four Jumbles, one letter to each square, to form four ordinary words.

YOSIN

LYDIO

TRYSAP

MUDINS

He'll never get anywhere acting like that

THIS MAY DETERMINE WHAT KIND OF POSITION YOU HAVE IN LIFE.

Answer: YOUR ⬡⬡⬡⬡⬡⬡⬡⬡⬡⬡⬡⬡⬡

JUMBLE®

Unscramble these four Jumbles, one letter to each square, to form four ordinary words.

INEEC

PRUCO

PEEXOS

SAHVNI

Lovely! I'll take three of them!

HE CALLED HER "DEAR" BEFORE MARRIAGE AND AFTERWARDS THIS.

Print answer here: " ⬡⬡⬡⬡⬡⬡⬡⬡⬡⬡ "

JUMBLE®

Unscramble these four Jumbles, one letter to each square, to form four ordinary words.

SOOGE

RAWGE

NAUCIV

JOUFLY

THAT BIG TALKER'S LISTENERS GOT NO CHANCE TO OPEN THEIR MOUTHS EXCEPT FOR THIS.

Print answer here: ⃝⃝⃝⃝⃝

JUMBLE®

Unscramble these four Jumbles, one letter to each
square, to form four ordinary words.

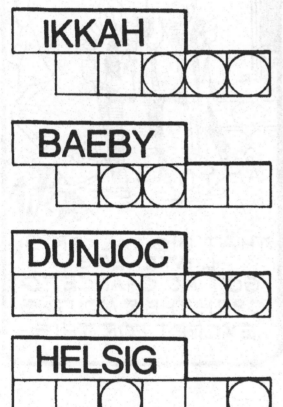

IKKAH

BAEBY

DUNJOC

HELSIG

Have you heard
the rumor
about him?

AN ACROBAT IS THE
ONLY PERSON WHO
CAN TALK ABOUT
HIMSELF THIS WAY.

Answer: ◯◯◯◯◯◯◯ HIS ◯◯◯◯
OWN

JUMBLE®

Unscramble these four Jumbles, one letter to each square, to form four ordinary words.

CAFTE

THAIB

DEPENX

REVOND

Doesn't make sense, but it's true

ANOTHER NAME FOR A MEDICAL PARTNERSHIP.

Print answer here: A

JUMBLE®

Unscramble these four Jumbles, one letter to each square, to form four ordinary words.

SARBS

NIRPT

FLUNGE

METIKS

You've got to learn to loosen up

WHAT THE SHRINK'S NERVOUS PATIENT WAS.

Answer here: " ◯◯◯◯◯ – ◯◯◯◯◯ "

106

JUMBLE®

Unscramble these four Jumbles, one letter to each
square, to form four ordinary words.

INARG

DYADD

YOBUDE

HIMSUL

WHY THE CROOK
DISGUISED HIMSELF
AS A SHEPHERD.

Answer: [ ][ ] WAS [ ][ ] THE " [ ][ ][ ][ ] "

JUMBLE®

Unscramble these four Jumbles, one letter to each square, to form four ordinary words.

HARCO

TISUE

DEDAHN

GIFNIX

I hope they've
got a job
for me

A—E

WHAT THE UNEM-
PLOYED BURLESQUE
DANCER HAD.

Answer: NO " ⬡⬡⬡⬡ " TO ⬡⬡⬡⬡⬡

JUMBLE®

Unscramble these four Jumbles, one letter to each square, to form four ordinary words.

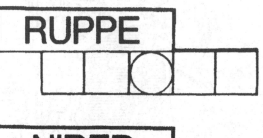

RUPPE

NIRED

GOTSDY

TIFFUL

SHE KNOWS
HOW TO GET
MORE OUT OF A
DRESS THAN THIS.

Answer here: SHE ◯◯◯◯◯ ◯◯◯◯◯ IT

JUMBLE®

Unscramble these four Jumbles, one letter to each square, to form four ordinary words.

ENMOY

USSOE

RIVLIE

MUPTIE

No hot water

No heat

Needs painting

THE LANDLORD'S PROMISES WERE NO BETTER THAN THIS.

Print answer here: HIS

JUMBLE®

Unscramble these four Jumbles, one letter to each square, to form four ordinary words.

OPYPP

RIPEV

NOPETT

GLAJEN

I can recall everything

WHAT A GOOD MEMORY REQUIRES.

Answer: ☐☐ ☐☐☐ OR ☐☐☐☐☐☐

JUMBLE®

Unscramble these four Jumbles, one letter to each square, to form four ordinary words.

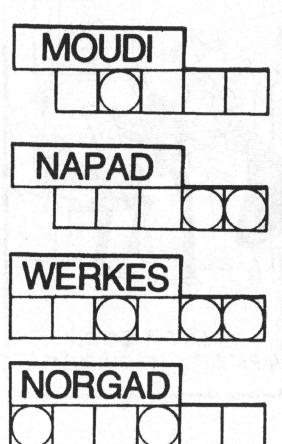

MOUDI

NAPAD

WERKES

NORGAD

HOW THEY FELT WHEN TEACHER GAVE A ZERO TO EVERYONE IN THE CLASS.

Answer here: "◯◯◯ – ◯◯◯◯◯◯◯"

JUMBLE®

Unscramble these four Jumbles, one letter to each
square, to form four ordinary words.

CUIJE

SOYUM

CLUDAN

DROPEN

HOW A GUY
USUALLY FINDS HIM-
SELF WHEN HE'S AL-
WAYS ASKING A-
ROUND FOR A LOAN.

Print answer here:

JUMBLE

Unscramble these four Jumbles, one letter to each square, to form four ordinary words.

NIVEL

RANOB

CHORCT

BLAMME

I wouldn't be caught dead in that filthy place

WHAT THEY CALLED THE REAR ENTRANCE OF THAT CAFETERIA.

Print answer here: THE

JUMBLE®

Unscramble these four Jumbles, one letter to each square, to form four ordinary words.

PIRAD

VEREF

KOOPHU

ARTUNI

WHAT THE LOAFER'S LIFE WORK WAS.

Print answer here: ⬡⬡ ⬡⬡⬡⬡⬡ IT

JUMBLE®

Unscramble these four Jumbles, one letter to each square, to form four ordinary words.

HINKT

KARNC

AMPODE

OXCIBE

He's studied the rules
very carefully

WHAT SAFE
DRIVING IS.

Answer here:

JUMBLE®

Unscramble these four Jumbles, one letter to each square, to form four ordinary words.

THERB

NEUSE

PEKUPE

EVVELT

WHAT HIS WIFE'S LITTLE POODLE WAS.

Print answer here: HIS ◯◯◯ ◯◯◯◯◯◯

JUMBLE®

Unscramble these four Jumbles, one letter to each square, to form four ordinary words.

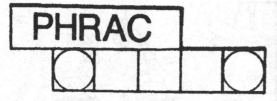

PHRAC

HILEW

TINKTE

CHIPUC

WHAT A MARRIAGE PROPOSAL IS.

Answer here: A ⬡⬡⬡⬡⬡ ⬡⬡⬡⬡⬡⬡

JUMBLE®

Unscramble these four Jumbles, one letter to each
square, to form four ordinary words.

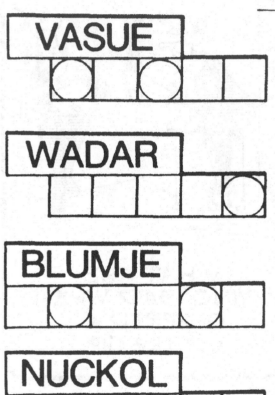

VASUE

WADAR

BLUMJE

NUCKOL

FOR AN OPINION
TO BE SOUND IT
MUST NOT BE THIS.

Print answer here:

JUMBLE®

Unscramble these four Jumbles, one letter to each square, to form four ordinary words.

RUHTT

SHIWK

HORKES

REALYY

WHAT THE
"WINO" SAID WHEN
OFFERED A
LITTLE SIP.

Print answer here: "  ,  "

JUMBLE®

Unscramble these four Jumbles, one letter to each
square, to form four ordinary words.

OJYLL

BOARR

TYBLUS

INTOOL

HOW "SHARP" REMARKS
MAY BE EXPRESSED,
ODDLY ENOUGH.

Print answer here:

JUMBLE

Unscramble these four Jumbles, one letter to each square, to form four ordinary words.

PIERG

GIHLT

DAHVEL

ANSTUE

WHAT HE SAID WHEN HE FELL INTO THE MANHOLE.

Answer here: "⬡⬡⬡⬡ ME A ⬡⬡⬡⬡"

JUMBLE®

Unscramble these four Jumbles, one letter to each square, to form four ordinary words.

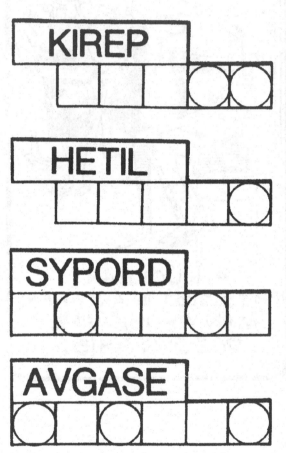

KIREP

HETIL

SYPORD

AVGASE

Awful

EDITOR

A POET WHO HOPES TO MAKE HIS LIVING FROM WRITING VERSES IS APT TO EXPERIENCE MANY OF THESE.

Print answer here:

JUMBLE®

Unscramble these four Jumbles, one letter to each square, to form four ordinary words.

UNGED

LINTE

GASYRS

DEPLUH

A NUCLEAR PHYSICIST IS ANOTHER MAN WHOSE WIFE DOESN'T THIS.

Answer here: ⬤⬤⬤⬤⬤⬤⬤⬤⬤⬤ HIM

Unscramble these four Jumbles, one letter to each square, to form four ordinary words.

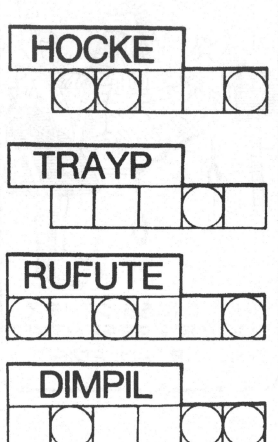

HOCKE

TRAYP

RUFUTE

DIMPIL

Regarding the economy . . .

AMERICA'S MOST OUTSTANDING PUBLIC FIGURE.

Answer here:

JUMBLE®

Unscramble these four Jumbles, one letter to each square, to form four ordinary words.

WATEK
◯◯ ◯◯

GEEBI
◯◯◯

DOMBEY
◯◯◯

SCAFAR
◯◯◯ ◯

WHY THOSE OTHER DOCTORS RESENTED THE ORTHOPEDIST.

Answer: HE ◯◯◯ ALL THE ◯◯◯◯◯◯

JUMBLE®

Unscramble these four Jumbles, one letter to each
square, to form four ordinary words.

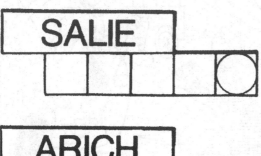

SALIE

ARICH

NALDIN

GOHMEA

Sounds like skullduggery
to me

WHAT THE
PHRENOLOGIST WAS.

Print answer here:

JUMBLE®

Unscramble these four Jumbles, one letter to each square, to form four ordinary words.

GOINJ

HAFES

FLIPER

SUMMUE

WHAT THE HEROIC FIREMAN BECAME.

Print answer here: " ◯◯◯◯◯ – ◯◯◯ "

JUMBLE®

Unscramble these four Jumbles, one letter to each square, to form four ordinary words.

KETOS

TIFED

DRAFTI

OSMACT

Makes my mouth water

RESTAURANT

Yum yum

PEOPLE WHO
LOVE SHELLFISH
BECOME HUNGRY
WHEN THEY DO THIS.

Print answer here: " ◯◯◯ " ◯◯◯◯◯

JUMBLE®

Unscramble these four Jumbles, one letter to each
square, to form four ordinary words.

ANGLD

HASAW

BRENAT

GURTIA

HOW THE WINNER
WAS CHOSEN
AT THAT BIG
ART CONTEST.

Print answer here: BY ☐ ☐☐☐☐☐☐☐☐

130

JUMBLE®

Unscramble these four Jumbles, one letter to each
square, to form four ordinary words.

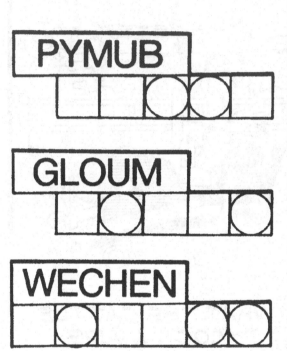

PYMUB

GLOUM

WECHEN

NALLEF

Go all
the way!

WHAT THEY THOUGHT
WHEN HE ROUNDED
SECOND BASE.

Answer: THERE'S NO 🔘🔘🔘🔘🔘 LIKE 🔘🔘🔘🔘

JUMBLE®

Unscramble these four Jumbles, one letter to each square, to form four ordinary words.

ASOBS

RIMPE

VOLJIA

NOOPUC

WHAT THE CATTLE TYCOON MADE A LOT OF.

Print answer here: " ☐☐☐ - ☐☐ "

JUMBLE®

Unscramble these four Jumbles, one letter to each square, to form four ordinary words.

HAMOC

NYKAL

THACED

MUTTUL

How about a higher one?

WHAT A CLIMB UP THAT LITTLE HILL DIDN'T DO.

Answer: "◯-◯◯◯◯◯◯" TO ◯◯◯◯◯

JUMBLE®

Unscramble these four Jumbles, one letter to each square, to form four ordinary words.

DOBOR

WICTE

CLAGEN

SMALID

WHAT THE SALES-
LADY SAID WHEN
ASKED WHETHER THAT
NEW TYPE FOUNDATION
GARMENT IS REALLY
GOING TO WORK.

Answer: " OF ☐☐☐☐☐ - ☐☐ " ☐☐☐☐☐

JUMBLE®

Unscramble these four Jumbles, one letter to each
square, to form four ordinary words.

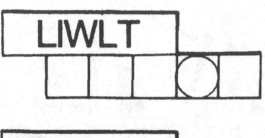

LIWLT

CYDUH

SAMOUF

RAAPPE

WHAT HAPPENED
WHEN THE SAFETY
MATCH TYCOON
LOST HIS TEMPER?

Print answer here: HE

135

JUMBLE®

Unscramble these four Jumbles, one letter to each square, to form four ordinary words.

GITHE

TRONS

THUBOG

OCTIXE

WHEN HIS TONGUE IS LOOSE, IT'S OFTEN BECAUSE HE IS THIS.

Print answer here: " ◯◯◯◯◯ "

JUMBLE®

Unscramble these four Jumbles, one letter to each
square, to form four ordinary words.

MACHP

PUJMY

RESTUM

BRUNKE

WHAT SHE DOES
WHEN SHE KISSES
HER HOCKEY
PLAYER BOYFRIEND.

Answer here: " ◯◯◯◯◯ - ◯◯◯◯ " ◯◯

JUMBLE®

Unscramble these four Jumbles, one letter to each square, to form four ordinary words.

IMDEG

NUDET

LETHAH

INGUMP

WHY THE FLOWER VENDOR WAS ARRESTED.

Answer here: FOR " ⬡⬡⬡⬡⬡ - ⬡⬡⬡ "

JUMBLE®

Unscramble these four Jumbles, one letter to each square, to form four ordinary words.

LENEK

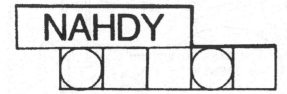
NAHDY

SYMFLE

TARIPE

WHAT THOSE CORDUROY PILLOWS MADE.

Print answer here:

JUMBLE®

Unscramble these four Jumbles, one letter to each square, to form four ordinary words.

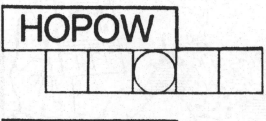

HOPOW

RABOX

JINTEC

MERMAH

Yes, sir . . .
No, sir . . .
Sorry, sir . . .
Won't happen
again, sir . . .

The old man is chewing him out

WHAT KIND OF A PROBLEM DID THE CAPTAIN FACE?

Answer here: A "◯◯◯◯◯" ◯◯◯

JUMBLE®

Unscramble these four Jumbles, one letter to each
square, to form four ordinary words.

INVEA

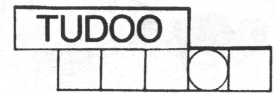

TUDOO

FARGOE

DIAMER

Nobody's called
me today

WHAT YOUR
TELEPHONE MIGHT
BECOME IF YOU FAIL
TO PAY THE BILL.

Answer here: A

141

JUMBLE®

Unscramble these four Jumbles, one letter to each square, to form four ordinary words.

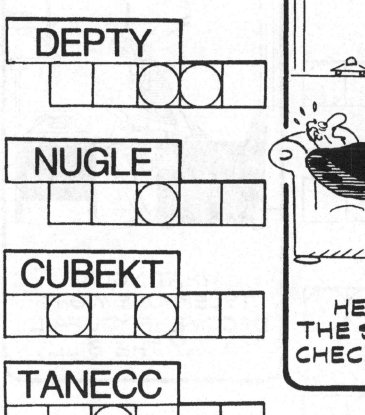

DEPTY

NUGLE

CUBEKT

TANECC

HE WENT TO THE SHRINK FOR A CHECKUP FOR THIS.

Print answer here: THE

JUMBLE®

Unscramble these four Jumbles, one letter to each
square, to form four ordinary words.

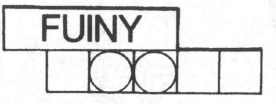

FUINY

BOESE

YATGIE

LAUMSY

WHY THE CARPENTER
NEEDED ALL
THAT EMERGENCY
DENTAL WORK.

Answer here: HE ◯◯◯ HIS ◯◯◯◯◯

143

JUMBLE®

Unscramble these four Jumbles, one letter to each square, to form four ordinary words.

DOYNS
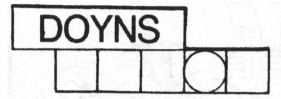

HOBAR

KOFERD
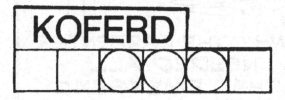

KALTEC
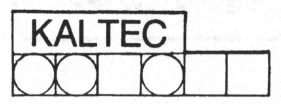

But I just wanted to go out for some air

WHY THE EMPLOYEE AT THE CAR FACTORY WAS FIRED.

Answer: HE ⬭⬭⬭⬭ A "⬭⬭⬭⬭⬭"

JUMBLE®

Unscramble these four Jumbles, one letter to each square, to form four ordinary words.

SIRUV

YOBOT

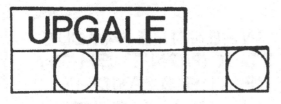

UPGALE

TAFOAL

THE BAKER HIRED—AND THEN FIRED—

Print answer here: A " ⬡⬡⬡⬡⬡ - ⬡⬡ "

JUMBLE®

Unscramble these four Jumbles, one letter to each square, to form four ordinary words.

GNUST

SHYKU

BUNNIO

YANTID

WHEN THE FAMOUS STAR DIDN'T SHOW UP, HIS STAND-IN BECAME THIS.

Print answer here: A ⬡⬡⬡⬡⬡⬡⬡⬡⬡

PUZZLE 145

JUMBLE®

Unscramble these four Jumbles, one letter to each square, to form four ordinary words.

RYCED

WEJEL

INGADE

NAULCY

THAT HAMMY MAGICIAN KNEW HOW TO MAKE THIS DISAPPEAR.

Print answer here: THE ⬡⬡⬡⬡⬡⬡⬡⬡⬡

JUMBLE®

Unscramble these four Jumbles, one letter to each square, to form four ordinary words.

DEBIP

TOMIF

DOGOLY

GURFAL

THE INSOMNIAC
WAS ADVISED
TO SLEEP ON THE
EDGE OF HIS BED
IN ORDER TO DO
THIS WITHOUT DELAY.

Print answer here: "◯◯◯◯◯ ◯◯◯"

JUMBLE®

Unscramble these four Jumbles, one letter to each square, to form four ordinary words.

REEMY

DESET

WILDEM

TRUIPY

WHAT A BELLY DANCER HAS TO KNOW HOW TO DO.

Answer: ⬡⬡⬡⬡⬡⬡⬡ HER "⬡⬡⬡"

JUMBLE®

Unscramble these four Jumbles, one letter to each square, to form four ordinary words.

YEGEL

ZIERP

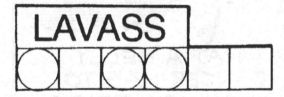

LAVASS

TRUFOH

WHEN YOU INVITE SOMEONE TO AN OUT-RAGEOUSLY EXPENSIVE RESTAURANT ——

Answer: IT ⬡⬡⬡⬡⬡⬡ YOU ⬡⬡⬡⬡⬡

JUMBLE®

Unscramble these four Jumbles, one letter to each square, to form four ordinary words.

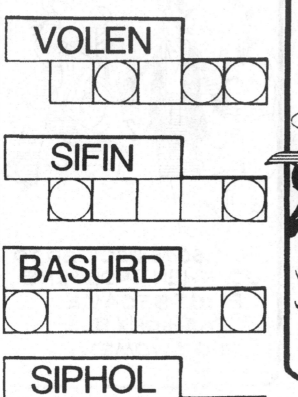

VOLEN

SIFIN

BASURD

SIPHOL

Bang

WHAT THE GUY WHO JUST PRETENDED HE WAS A GANGSTER MUST HAVE BEEN.

Answer here: A " ◯◯◯◯◯ ◯◯◯◯ "

JUMBLE®

Unscramble these four Jumbles, one letter to each square, to form four ordinary words.

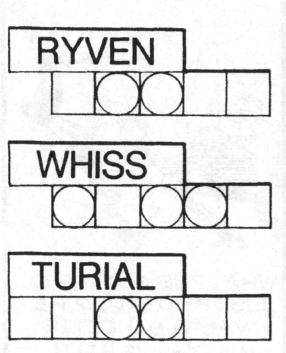

RYVEN

WHISS

TURIAL

SCYTIK

Wouldn't be caught dead in them

WHAT SOME DECIDED TO DO WHEN TROUSERS FIRST BECAME FASHIONABLE FOR WOMEN.

Answer: ☐☐☐☐☐ THE ☐☐☐☐☐

JUMBLE®

Unscramble these four Jumbles, one letter to each square, to form four ordinary words.

KRYJE

DYPUG

TULNAW

YENNIT

Nobody goes there anymore

EATS

WHAT THE SLEAZY RESTAURANT THAT MADE THOSE AWFUL SUBMARINE SAND-WICHES DID.

Print answer here:

153

PUZZLE
152

JUMBLE®

Unscramble these four Jumbles, one letter to each
square, to form four ordinary words.

VOYIR

TOINX

KLEECH

ETSAUL

WHY THE JUDGE
COULDN'T BE DIS-
TURBED AT DINNER.

Answer: HIS [◯◯◯◯◯] WAS " [◯◯◯◯◯◯] "
AT

154

JUMBLE®

Unscramble these four Jumbles, one letter to each
square, to form four ordinary words.

NARVE

IRROP

EMBLUH

PECDIT

THE BARBER TOLD
HIM STORIES THAT
COULD DO THIS.

Print answer here: ⬡⬡⬡⬡ HIS ⬡⬡⬡⬡

JUMBLE®

Unscramble these four Jumbles, one letter to each
square, to form four ordinary words.

IMNEC

CUPAN

KORSEM

SIMPOE

I am authorized to . . .

WHEN THEY
WANTED TO FIND
OUT ABOUT THE BIG
BICYCLE MERGER, THEY
INTERVIEWED THIS.

Answer: THE " ⬡⬡⬡⬡⬡⬡⬡ – ⬡⬡⬡ "

JUMBLE®

Unscramble these four Jumbles, one letter to each square, to form four ordinary words.

OIXED

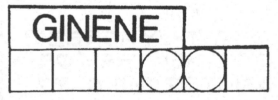

BOREP

GINENE

MADGEA

WHAT THE MAESTRO CALLED HIS ASSISTANT.

Answer here: HIS "   "

JUMBLE®

Unscramble these four Jumbles, one letter to each square, to form four ordinary words.

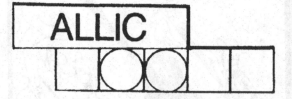

ALLIC

THYAS

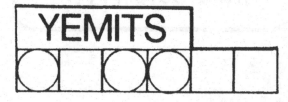

CYRIKT

YEMITS

WHAT THEY AGREED TO WHEN THEY OR-GANIZED THE CARD GAME ON THE PLANE.

Answer: THE ⬡⬡⬡'⬡ THE ⬡⬡⬡⬡⬡⬡

JUMBLE®

Unscramble these four Jumbles, one letter to each
square, to form four ordinary words.

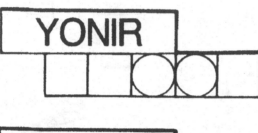

YONIR

PEXLE

POWDLE

YUGLIT

WHAT HAPPENED WHEN
THE PRICE OF DUCK
FEATHERS INCREASED?

Print answer here:  WENT

JUMBLE®

Unscramble these four Jumbles, one letter to each
square, to form four ordinary words.

LITTE

ITTYD

DARZIL

OPEATT

WHAT THE GOSSIPY
RATTLESNAKE WAS.

Answer: A ◯◯◯◯◯◯ " ◯◯◯◯ "

JUMBLE

Unscramble these four Jumbles, one letter to each square, to form four ordinary words.

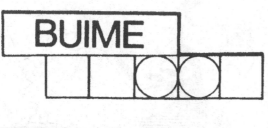

BUIME

SHUBY

RATROM

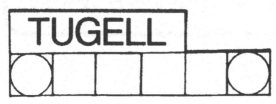

TUGELL

ANOTHER NAME FOR A PIRATE SHIP.

Answer here: A " ⬡⬡⬡⬡ " ⬡⬡⬡⬡

JUMBLE®

Unscramble these four Jumbles, one letter to each square, to form four ordinary words.

CHEFT

ILLSE

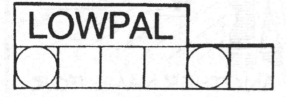
LOWPAL

TAUNER

WHAT THAT PRIZE-WINNING DOG WAS.

Print answer here: A ◯◯◯◯◯ "◯◯◯"

JUMBLE®

Fiesta

Challenger Puzzles

JUMBLE®

Unscramble these six Jumbles, one letter to each square, to form six ordinary words.

SEATTE

NOCABE

WEFTES

PYGINT

HANVEE

DACUDE

A GREAT COMPOSER INVOLVED WITH SURGERY.

PRINT YOUR ANSWER IN THE CIRCLES BELOW

AN ◯◯◯◯◯◯◯◯◯◯◯

JUMBLE®

Unscramble these six Jumbles, one letter to each square, to form six ordinary words.

LOVVEE

INLOOT

CAEPIE

GRIFIN

TRAPCE

BEBJOR

ANOTHER NAME FOR A WIG.

PRINT YOUR ANSWER IN THE CIRCLES BELOW

A ◯◯◯◯◯◯◯◯◯◯◯ ◯◯◯

JUMBLE®

Unscramble these six Jumbles, one letter to each square, to form six ordinary words.

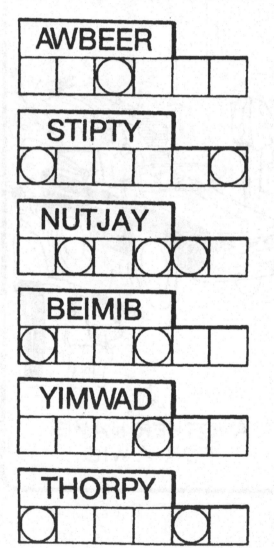

AWBEER

STIPTY

NUTJAY

BEIMIB

YIMWAD

THORPY

He thinks he's being funny

BAR

WHAT A TAUNT MIGHT BE.

PRINT YOUR ANSWER IN THE CIRCLES BELOW

MORE ☐☐☐☐☐ ☐☐☐☐☐ ☐☐☐

JUMBLE®

Unscramble these six Jumbles, one letter to each square, to form six ordinary words.

TARRMY

YURGAS

REPJUM

SHUCOR

CHYPIS

TOPITE

WHAT A SUCCESSFUL BOXER HAS TO CONSIDER.

PRINT YOUR ANSWER IN THE CIRCLES BELOW

THE " ☐☐☐☐☐☐ " OF ☐☐☐☐☐☐

JUMBLE

Unscramble these six Jumbles, one letter to each square, to form six ordinary words.

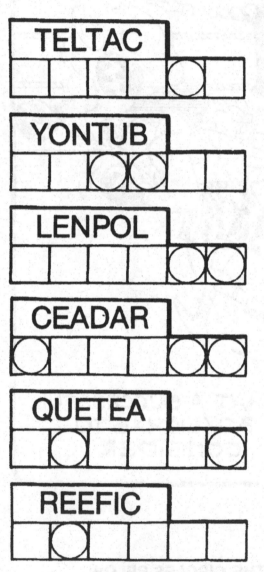

TELTAC

YONTUB

LENPOL

CEADAR

QUETEA

REEFIC

I'll wait until that Roman comes

WHEN CLEOPATRA KEPT SAYING NO, THEY CALLED HER THIS.

PRINT YOUR ANSWER IN THE CIRCLES BELOW

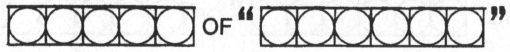

OF " "

JUMBLE

Unscramble these six Jumbles, one letter to each square, to form six ordinary words.

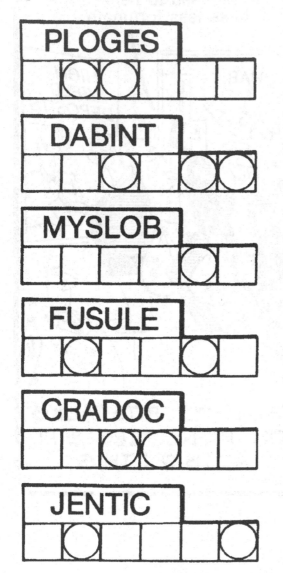

PLOGES

DABINT

MYSLOB

FUSULE

CRADOC

JENTIC

He made a hurried judgment

Should have taken lessons first

HOW SOME SKIERS HAVE BEEN KNOWN TO JUMP.

PRINT YOUR ANSWER IN THE CIRCLES BELOW

JUMBLE®

Unscramble these six Jumbles, one letter to each square, to form six ordinary words.

MOARFT

CEITED

VINTAY

TIFISM

WOBELL

YAWNAY

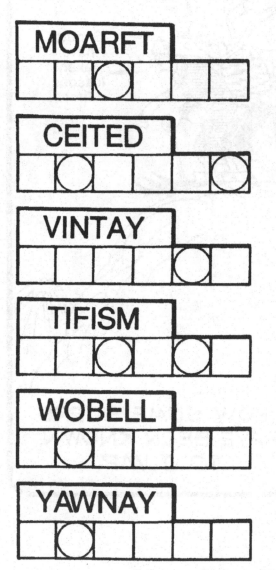

I say that money should be used to help those less fortunate

BANK

HIGH YIELD DEPOSITS

THE HYPOCRITE TALKS ON "PRINCIPLES" BUT ACTS ON THIS.

PRINT YOUR ANSWER IN THE CIRCLES BELOW

"◯◯◯◯◯◯◯◯◯"

JUMBLE

Unscramble these six Jumbles, one letter to each
square, to form six ordinary words.

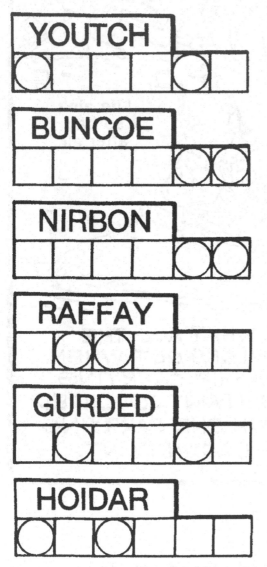

YOUTCH

BUNCOE

NIRBON

RAFFAY

GURDED

HOIDAR

HOW DOES A
MONSTER LIKE HIS
POTATOES?

PRINT YOUR ANSWER IN THE CIRCLES BELOW

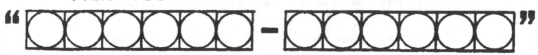

" ⬡⬡⬡⬡⬡⬡⬡ – ⬡⬡⬡⬡⬡⬡ "

JUMBLE®

Unscramble these six Jumbles, one letter to each square, to form six ordinary words.

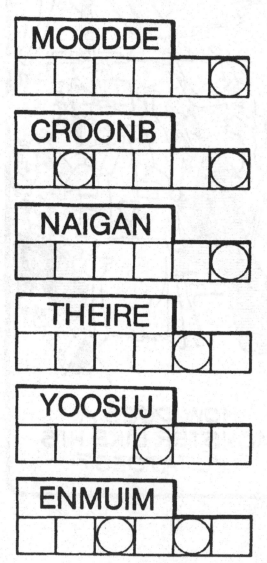

MOODDE

CROONB

NAIGAN

THEIRE

YOOSUJ

ENMUIM

Life ain't so bad after all

WHAT ALL THE SAILORS GOT WHEN A SHIP CARRYING RED PAINT COLLIDED WITH ONE CARRYING BROWN PAINT.

PRINT YOUR ANSWER IN THE CIRCLES BELOW

" ◯◯◯◯◯◯◯◯◯ "

JUMBLE®

Unscramble these six Jumbles, one letter to each square, to form six ordinary words.

NODARP

YOMARR

BONKER

YEMBOR

LUCASE

GROITE

They're both a couple of dogs as far as I'm concerned

WHAT PRESIDENTIAL "TIMBER" IS OFTEN COMPOSED OF.

PRINT YOUR ANSWER IN THE CIRCLES BELOW

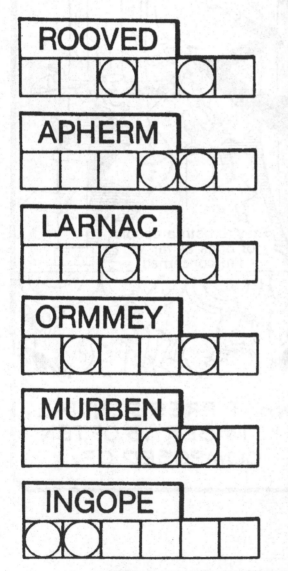

JUMBLE®

Unscramble these six Jumbles, one letter to each square, to form six ordinary words.

ROOVED

APHERM

LARNAC

ORMMEY

MURBEN

INGOPE

WHAT THE BOY SCOUT SAID WHEN HE FIXED THE HORN ON THE LITTLE OLD LADY'S BICYCLE.

PRINT YOUR ANSWER IN THE CIRCLES BELOW

" ⬡⬡⬡⬡⬡ ⬡⬡⬡⬡⬡⬡⬡⬡⬡ "

JUMBLE®

Unscramble these six Jumbles, one letter to each square, to form six ordinary words.

DEMOAP

NURYGH

SIGAHR

DOAJIN

BILBEN

ENCOSH

There goes the environment!

WHAT THEY CALLED THE GANGSTER WHO MOVED NEXT DOOR.

PRINT YOUR ANSWER IN THE CIRCLES BELOW

THE " ☐☐☐☐☐☐☐☐ ☐☐☐☐ "

JUMBLE

Unscramble these six Jumbles, one letter to each square, to form six ordinary words.

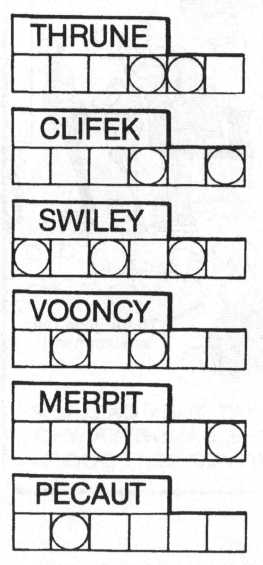

THRUNE

CLIFEK

SWILEY

VOONCY

MERPIT

PECAUT

WHEN DID A DOZEN SWIMMERS TAKE THE PLUNGE?

PRINT YOUR ANSWER IN THE CIRCLES BELOW

AT THE ◯◯◯◯◯◯ OF ◯◯◯◯◯◯

JUMBLE

Unscramble these six Jumbles, one letter to each
square, to form six ordinary words.

CLINPE

BLOMIE

GRATTE

TOORRA

HUBBYC

DARFOE

A CAT ATE CHEESE
AND WAITED FOR THE
MOUSE WITH THIS.

PRINT YOUR ANSWER IN THE CIRCLES BELOW

JUMBLE®

Unscramble these six Jumbles, one letter to each square, to form six ordinary words.

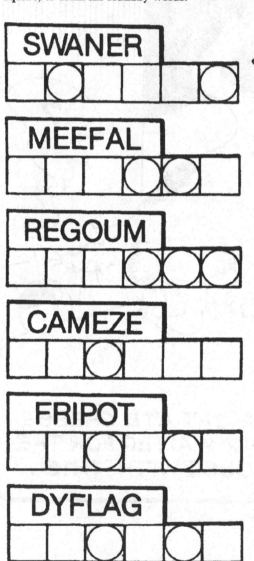

SWANER

MEEFAL

REGOUM

CAMEZE

FRIPOT

DYFLAG

WHAT THEY CALLED THE ALLIGATOR WHO STROLLED INTO THE HOTEL LOBBY.

PRINT YOUR ANSWER IN THE CIRCLES BELOW

A " ◯◯◯◯◯ ◯◯◯◯◯◯◯ "

JUMBLE®

Unscramble these six Jumbles, one letter to each square, to form six ordinary words.

MISOGE

RESPON

NAHLED

FORREV

SIMYAD

INSECK

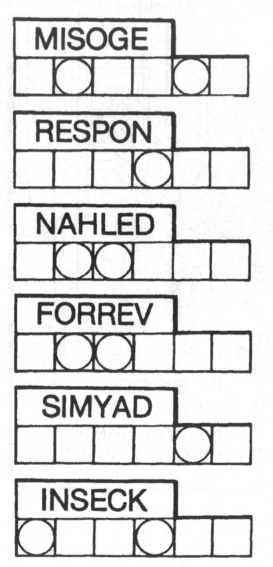

I wouldn't trust a man who talks out of both sides of his mouth at the same time

WHAT A MAN WHO SPEAKS WITH FORKED TONGUE PROBABLY IS.

PRINT YOUR ANSWER IN THE CIRCLES BELOW

A ☐☐☐☐☐☐ IN THE ☐☐☐☐☐

JUMBLE®

Unscramble these six Jumbles, one letter to each square, to form six ordinary words.

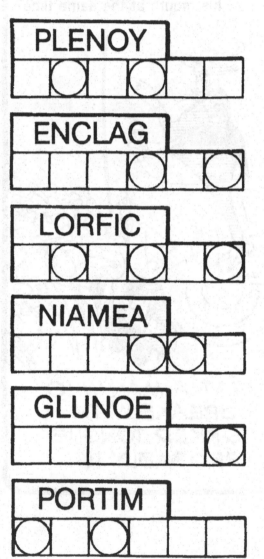

PLENOY

ENCLAG

LORFIC

NIAMEA

GLUNOE

PORTIM

That's Washington, surrounded by Adams, Jefferson and Hamilton

IN GOOD GOVERNMENT, THE PRINCIPAL MEN SHOULD BE THIS.

PRINT YOUR ANSWER IN THE CIRCLES BELOW

OF

JUMBLE®

Unscramble these six Jumbles, one letter to each square, to form six ordinary words.

GREEME

RATVAC

BAILUR

TINVER

SHAUTI

DROMEN

WHAT KIND OF A CONFERENCE IS THIS, APPARENTLY?

PRINT YOUR ANSWER IN THE CIRCLES BELOW

" ◯◯◯◯◯◯◯◯◯◯◯◯ "

JUMBLE®

Unscramble these six Jumbles, one letter to each square, to form six ordinary words.

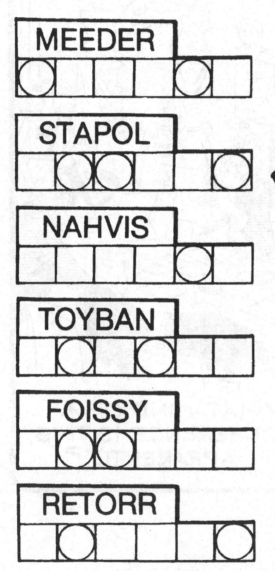

MEEDER

STAPOL

NAHVIS

TOYBAN

FOISSY

RETORR

HOW MOST DEFEATED PRIZE-FIGHTERS LEAVE THE RING.

PRINT YOUR ANSWER IN THE CIRCLES BELOW

JUMBLE

Unscramble these six Jumbles, one letter to each
square, to form six ordinary words.

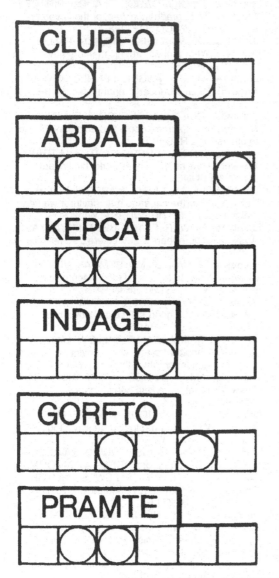

CLUPEO

ABDALL

KEPCAT

INDAGE

GORFTO

PRAMTE

AN EVENING DRESS
IS SOMETIMES DE-
SIGNED TO HELP THE
WEARER CATCH THIS.

PRINT YOUR ANSWER IN THE CIRCLES BELOW

ANSWERS

1. **Jumbles:** SWISH IGLOO HANGAR EITHER
   Answer: What the guard at the haunted house said—WHO GHOST THERE?

2. **Jumbles:** SKULK GULLY JOBBER SAVAGE
   Answer: What those ants at the picnic do—"BUG" US

3. **Jumbles:** SMACK CRAZY PRIMED NOODLE
   Answer: What happened when he accidently pulled the altitude stick?—IT MADE HIM "SOAR"

4. **Jumbles:** JOLLY CHAFF DECODE PESTLE
   Answer: What the guy who hid his wallet in the freezer was left with—COLD CASH

5. **Jumbles:** VOUCH INKED ARCTIC FOMENT
   Answer: Better not make this kind of homemade bread—COUNTERFEIT

6. **Jumbles:** DUMPY FRANC ORCHID BEAUTY
   Answer: What the guy who got stuck in the revolving door doesn't get anymore—AROUND MUCH

7. **Jumbles:** CURIO BARGE NAPKIN MATURE
   Answer: What some skaters might have to do in order to get better acquainted—BREAK THE ICE

8. **Jumbles:** RODEO IDIOM CRABBY INJURY
   Answer: He decided to watch his drinking—by only visiting bars that have this—A MIRROR

9. **Jumbles:** GRIPE POISE JACKAL PEWTER
   Answer: What the judge gave the guy who was arrested for stealing a watch—THE "WORKS"

10. **Jumbles:** SNARL DRAMA ACCESS HALVED
    Answer: What the guy who was "all feet" when he danced was when they sat down—ALL HANDS

11. **Jumbles:** LEGAL BOOTH ADRIFT MARROW
    Answer: What the blind date she was looking forward to meeting turned out to be—A "DREAM BLOAT"

12. **Jumbles:** RHYME AUDIT HAMPER FRENZY
    Answer: If she ever told her real age, her birthday cake would be this—A FIRE HAZARD

13. **Jumbles:** APRON WRATH ELDEST BURLAP
    Answer: In order to find out which kind of ice-cream soda is the best, take this—A "STRAW" POLL

14. **Jumbles:** DOUGH GLOVE MOBILE INCOME
    Answer: Needed to impress a laundress—A GOOD LINE

15. **Jumbles:** PRIME DIZZY SUPERB JUMPER
    Answer: What he often did behind his wife's back—ZIPPED HER UP

16. **Jumbles:** FLOUR AGING INTACT LEDGER
    Answer: Her face is her fortune, and it runs into this—A NICE FIGURE

17. **Jumbles:** BRAVE HONEY ANYHOW CUDGEL
    Answer: He had a "peach" of a secretary until his wife ordered this—HER "CANNED"

18. **Jumbles:** CRIME AISLE CACTUS KNOTTY
    Answer: Could it be a raincoat for wear in the big town?—A CITY SLICKER

19. **Jumbles:** APART SCARF LIQUID CHARGE
    Answer: Some people keep trying on shoes until the salesman does this—HAS A FIT

20. **Jumbles:** EXILE VIRUS MUSCLE LEGACY
    Answer: How far down was her bathing suit cut?—TO "SEE" LEVEL

21. **Jumbles:** DROOP WHILE MUSLIN TOWARD
    Answer: Why the business tycoon rushed off on a much needed vacation—TO SLOW DOWN

22. **Jumbles:** BIRCH CLOUT FELONY HIDING
    Answer: Why his ex-wife took him to the cleaners—HE WAS FILTHY RICH

23. **Jumbles:** FETCH TRAIT EXPEND TURKEY
    Answer: What he and his girl were—PRETTY THICK

24. **Jumbles:** GUILT HITCH MORGUE HELMET
    Answer: What the invisible man's wife saw when her husband gave his usual lame excuse—RIGHT THROUGH HIM

25. **Jumbles:** RIGOR NUDGE OPENLY ARTFUL
    Answer: They resented that ritzy pooch because he always wanted to do this—PUT ON THE DOG

26. **Jumbles:** BANJO HEFTY JACKAL SIZZLE
    Answer: What a coward might do when he gets into a "jam"—SHAKE LIKE JELLY

27. **Jumbles:** BEFIT OWING SPORTY ACCORD
    Answer: Regardless of what the orchestra performs, the bass player has to do this—STAND FOR IT

28. **Jumbles:** SOUSE NOISY FEDORA CHROME
    Answer: Why the game warden didn't believe his story—IT SEEMED FISHY

29. **Jumbles:** MINER LUNGE UPLIFT BARIUM
    Answer: What the young photographer thought the lighting lesson was—ILLUMINATING

30. **Jumbles:** BRASS HURRY SPLEEN POLITE
    Answer: To get good at climbing you must—LEARN THE ROPES

31. **Jumbles:** SMOKY GAUGE FLAGON PIRACY
    Answer: What graduation was for those young people—THE "PROM" OF LIFE

32. **Jumbles:** DELVE FLUKE ARMADA PALLID
    Answer: What a photographic memory never seems to run out of—FILM

33. **Jumbles:** GLORY AUGUR FENNEL PHYSIC
    Answer: What a dancer's reputation often rests upon—HER LEGS

34. **Jumbles:** GUILE BASIN FLORID EXCITE
    Answer: Food some people find edible might seem this to others—INCREDIBLE

35. **Jumbles:** CROAK SUEDE PANTRY HOTBED
    Answer: How an osteopath works his fingers—TO *YOUR* BONES

36. **Jumbles:** BULLY LATHE MARROW WALRUS
    Answer: How the sausage manufacturer wanted to make money—IN THE "WURST" WAY

37. **Jumbles:** BOWER FLANK BECALM ZINNIA
    Answer: Where there's a will there's sometimes this—A WAIL

38. **Jumbles:** PECAN BLIMP BEMOAN VISION
    Answer: The jogger visited the veterinarian because of this—HIS "CALVES" WERE IN PAIN

39. **Jumbles:** PROVE OLDER HIATUS SECEDE
    Answer: What a good salesman knows how to bring—ORDERS OUT OF CHAOS

40. **Jumbles:** GRIMY CHANT TALLOW SWERVE
    Answer: People who are too anxious to make a living have sometimes forgotten this—HOW TO LIVE

41. **Jumbles:** AMITY DUNCE SLUICE MURMUR
    Answer: What the organ grinder had—A "TURN" FOR MUSIC

42. **Jumbles:** FOAMY JUDGE WHEEZE MATRON
    Answer: Where the geology professor brought his students—DOWN TO EARTH

43. **Jumbles:** PLAID MOUSE INNING SAVORY
    Answer: What an optometrist is—A MAN OF VISION

44. **Jumbles:** TIGER GNOME FEWEST BLUISH
    Answer: Every time baby cried they gave him this—THE "WHINE" BOTTLE

45. **Jumbles:** COLON NOBLE SQUALL TORRID
    Answer: A woman goes to a hair stylist when she doesn't want to show this—HER TRUE COLORS

46. **Jumbles:** CYCLE PUPIL HAUNCH MAYHEM
    Answer: He'll never break his word in a love letter, except with this—A HYPHEN

47. **Jumbles:** WEIGH FLOUR INBORN BEHELD
    Answer: He picked a soft job because he expected to do this later—LIE DOWN ON IT

48. **Jumbles:** PAPER GLEAM DARING BLOUSE
    Answer: How a pastry chef doesn't live—BY BREAD ALONE

49. **Jumbles:** CYNIC PIECE OUTFIT GAMBOL
Answer: What sort of job do they do delivering parcels?—A "BANG-UP" ONE

50. **Jumbles:** CHIME MOOSE DEBATE SURTAX
Answer: What a politician's life often is—
A BED OF "RUSES"

51. **Jumbles:** LYRIC GAUZE CLOVEN FACING
Answer: What you will never have if you fall in love with yourself—A RIVAL

52. **Jumbles:** LOUSY STAID HEIFER TONGUE
Answer: In Germany, it might provide the answer to the common cold—"GESUNDHEIT"

53. **Jumbles:** TASTY GRIME SHAKEN ORIGIN
Answer: How a warmonger believes in talking—
WITH HIS ARMS

54. **Jumbles:** NUTTY WHEEL OMELET BABOON
Answer: What happens when you slip on thin ice?—
YOUR BOTTOM GETS "THAW"

55. **Jumbles:** MILKY GAVEL SONATA TIMING
Answer: He had the self-control to give up drinking and smoking but not the self-control to give up this—
TALKING ABOUT IT

56. **Jumbles:** DOUSE IDIOT ABSORB SHEKEL
Answer: What a self-employed person is never apt to do—DISLIKE THE BOSS

57. **Jumbles:** KITTY LOGIC JOBBER ABACUS
Answer: What two wrongs sometimes actually do make—A "RIOT"

58. **Jumbles:** MINUS SCOUR VOYAGE PURPLE
Answer: If it sounds like a "whine," it's probably a complaint that comes from this—SOUR GRAPES

59. **Jumbles:** KNOWN HAZEL EQUITY COUGAR
Answer: The next-door neighbor who's always borrowing your stuff will take anything from you except this—A HINT

60. **Jumbles:** GOUGE QUILT MELODY SEETHE
Answer: What a mean man who would steal candy from a baby is—A HEEL WITHOUT A "SOUL"

61. **Jumbles:** CAKED REBEL BARREN DISOWN
Answer: A pessimist is always good for this—
BAD NEWS

62. **Jumbles:** MESSY COACH BUREAU MISERY
Answer: What the bridge on the violin enables the player to get—HIS MUSIC "ACROSS"

63. **Jumbles:** TYING NOTCH MISUSE VALISE
Answer: What the boy snake said to the girl snake—
GIVE US A HISS

64. **Jumbles:** GULLY RAINY CARBON POETRY
Answer: Napoleon was the first man who thought he was this—NAPOLEON

65. **Jumbles:** MADLY WEARY FIZZLE JINGLE
Answer: Formerly found only in the country but now commonly seen in the city—WILD LIFE

66. **Jumbles:** SLANT HUMAN VIOLIN WOEFUL
Answer: What the bigamist would like to keep—
"TWO" HIMSELF

67. **Jumbles:** AWOKE MINOR DRUDGE PIGPEN
Answer: Another name for a philanderer—
A DAME DROPPER

68. **Jumbles:** MOUND GUMBO MUTTON BYGONE
Answer: What somebody who tries to please everybody is apt to remain—A NOBODY

69. **Jumbles:** FOLIO VIGIL BOBBIN GROUCH
Answer: What were Alexander Graham Bell's first words?—GOO GOO

70. **Jumbles:** WEDGE BRAND LIKELY PEWTER
Answer: What the hypochondriac was sick of—
BEING WELL

71. **Jumbles:** BARGE LEAFY TYRANT HOURLY
Answer: What they called her husband who was addicted to gambling—HER "BETTOR" HALF

72. **Jumbles:** CLEFT GUIDE DONKEY FLAXEN
Answer: A day off is sometimes followed by this—
AN OFF DAY

73. **Jumbles:** TOXIC YACHT HUNGRY CURFEW
Answer: What the road hog believes "might" makes—
RIGHT-OF WAY

74. **Jumbles:** MOURN UTTER LAYOFF POWDER
Answer: What yeast is—FLOUR POWER

75. **Jumbles:** LEAVE MAJOR CROUCH BUTTER
Answer: What the outlaws turned skydivers had—
A "CHUTE" OUT

76. **Jumbles:** FOYER YEARN SYSTEM HEARTH
Answer: A person who always borrows trouble is usually anxious to do this—
SHARE IT WITH OTHERS

77. **Jumbles:** LEGAL IRATE BRANDY RABBIT
Answer: Another name for sarcasm—BARBED "IRE"

78. **Jumbles:** WOMEN IDIOM GHETTO JOSTLE
Answer: He lies in wait for a fish, and after catching it he does this—LIES IN WEIGHT

79. **Jumbles:** PIETY WAFER GOLFER THRIVE
Answer: What the bus driver told him—
WHERE TO GET OFF

80. **Jumbles:** DERBY JOUST DAMASK POLLEN
Answer: A woman can say more in a look than a man can in this—A BOOK

81. **Jumbles:** FILMY CRESS OUTING THWART
Answer: On a blind date he was expecting a "vision," but it turned out to be this—A "SIGHT"

82. **Jumbles:** MIRTH ITCHY UPWARD HEARSE
Answer: One way to save face is to learn to keep this—PART OF IT SHUT

83. **Jumbles:** GIANT AROMA CHORUS DILUTE
Answer: If a job is to have a future, it's likely to depend on this—THE MAN WHO HOLDS IT

84. **Jumbles:** FAINT PHOTO DREDGE STYLUS
Answer: A guy who's always boasting about his family tree probably comes from this—ITS SHADY SIDE

85. **Jumbles:** FRAME HITCH BOUNCE ABUSED
Answer: She has what it takes to wear the latest fashions—A RICH HUSBAND

86. **Jumbles:** BRAVE LOWLY GADFLY HUNTER
Answer: That windbag was always getting carried away by the sound of his own voice, but never this—
FAR ENOUGH

87. **Jumbles:** UNCLE LYING PRAYER INVEST
Answer: How the undertaker presented his bill—
GRAVELY

88. **Jumbles:** EATEN FENCE HINDER DETAIN
Answer: Goliath was surprised by what David did because such a thing had never this before—
ENTERED HIS HEAD

89. **Jumbles:** TOOTH COUPE KILLER VANDAL
Answer: She was never overlooked, but usually this—
LOOKED OVER

90. **Jumbles:** OAKEN MERGE POSTAL NUMBER
Answer: A person who wakes up to find himself famous may not have this—BEEN ASLEEP

91. **Jumbles:** FRAUD PATIO DAMPEN LOCALE
Answer: That visitor who drops in for a call might actually be wanting to do this—CALL IN FOR A DROP

92. **Jumbles:** TRILL DIZZY KIDNAP LATEST
Answer: What there was a lot of at the unemployment office—"IDLE" TALK

93. **Jumbles:** BATCH JOKER LIQUID PURVEY
Answer: When the kids have to play in on account of bad weather the parents often end up this way—
PLAYED OUT

94. **Jumbles:** DROOP LARVA SURELY CIPHER
Answer: What the intellectual hobo was—
A ROAD SCHOLAR

185

95. **Jumbles:** QUAKE TARDY MUSCLE PAGODA
Answer: A blaze can be very hot, especially when it's this—"COALED"

96. **Jumbles:** MOUTH APART LADING NETHER
Answer: What a woman might attempt to draw with an eyebrow pencil—ATTENTION

97. **Jumbles:** BANDY TEMPO DULCET CHEERY
Answer: What the "ham" was for the drama critic—HIS "MEAT"

98. **Jumbles:** PYLON FUDGE CASHEW DITHER
Answer: A girl who now tells him where to take her might later tell him this—WHERE TO GO

99. **Jumbles:** NOISY DOILY PASTRY NUDISM
Answer: This may determine what kind of position you have in life—YOUR DISPOSITION

100. **Jumbles:** NIECE CROUP EXPOSE VANISH
Answer: He called her "dear" before marriage and afterwards this—"EXPENSIVE"

101. **Jumbles:** GOOSE WAGER VICUNA JOYFUL
Answer: That big talker's listeners got no chance to open their mouths except for this—YAWNS

102. **Jumbles:** KHAKI ABBEY JOCUND SLEIGH
Answer: An acrobat is the only person who can talk about himself this way—BEHIND HIS OWN BACK

103. **Jumbles:** FACET HABIT EXPEND VENDOR
Answer: Another name for a medical partnership—A PARADOX

104. **Jumbles:** BRASS PRINT ENGULF KISMET
Answer: What the shrink's nervous patient was—"SELF-TAUT"

105. **Jumbles:** GRAIN DADDY BUOYED MULISH
Answer: Why the crook disguised himself as a shepherd—HE WAS ON THE "LAMB"

106. **Jumbles:** ROACH SUITE HANDED FIXING
Answer: What the unemployed burlesque dancer had—NO "ACTS" TO GRIND

107. **Jumbles:** UPPER DINER STODGY FITFUL
Answer: She knows how to get more out of a dress than this—SHE PUTS INTO IT

108. **Jumbles:** MONEY SOUSE VIRILE IMPUTE
Answer: The landlord's promises were no better than this—HIS PREMISES

109. **Jumbles:** POPPY VIPER POTENT JANGLE
Answer: What a good memory requires—NO PEN OR PAPER

110. **Jumbles:** ODIUM PANDA SKEWER DRAGON
Answer: How they felt when teacher gave a zero to everyone in the class—"DE-GRADED"

111. **Jumbles:** JUICE MOUSY UNCLAD PONDER
Answer: How a guy usually finds himself when he's always asking around for a loan—ALONE

112. **Jumbles:** LIVEN BARON CROTCH EMBALM
Answer: What they called the rear entrance of that cafeteria—THE BACTERIA

113. **Jumbles:** RAPID FEVER HOOKUP NUTRIA
Answer: What the loafer's life work was—TO AVOID IT

114. **Jumbles:** THINK CRANK POMADE ICEBOX
Answer: What safe driving is—NO ACCIDENT

115. **Jumbles:** BERTH ENSUE UPKEEP VELVET
Answer: What his wife's little poodle was—HIS PET PEEVE

116. **Jumbles:** PARCH WHILE KITTEN HICCUP
Answer: What a marriage proposal is—A HITCH PITCH

117. **Jumbles:** SUAVE AWARD JUMBLE UNLOCK
Answer: For an opinion to be sound it must not be this—ALL SOUND

118. **Jumbles:** TRUTH WHISK KOSHER YEARLY
Answer: What the "wino" said when offered a little sip—"WHY, YES"

119. **Jumbles:** JOLLY ARBOR SUBTLY LOTION
Answer: How "sharp" remarks may be expressed, oddly enough—BLUNTLY

120. **Jumbles:** GRIPE LIGHT HALVED UNSEAT
Answer: What he said when he fell into the manhole—"GIVE ME A HAND"

121. **Jumbles:** PIKER LITHE DROPSY SAVAGE
Answer: A poet who hopes to make his living from writing verses is apt to experience many of these—REVERSES

122. **Jumbles:** NUDGE INLET GRASSY UPHELD
Answer: A nuclear physicist is another man whose wife doesn't this—UNDERSTAND HIM

123. **Jumbles:** CHOKE PARTY FUTURE LIMPID
Answer: America's most outstanding public figure—THE DEFICIT

124. **Jumbles:** TWEAK BEIGE EMBODY FRACAS
Answer: Why those other doctors resented the orthopedist—HE GOT ALL THE BREAKS

125. **Jumbles:** AISLE CHAIR INLAND HOMAGE
Answer: What the phrenologist was—HEAD MAN

126. **Jumbles:** JINGO SHEAF PILFER MUSEUM
Answer: What the heroic fireman became—"FLAM-OUS"

127. **Jumbles:** STOKE FETID ADRIFT MASCOT
Answer: People who love shellfish become hungry when they do this—"SEA" FOOD

128. **Jumbles:** GLAND AWASH BANTER GUITAR
Answer: How the winner was chosen at the big art contest—BY A DRAWING

129. **Jumbles:** BUMPY MOGUL WHENCE FALLEN
Answer: What they thought when he rounded second base—THERE'S NO PLACE LIKE HOME

130. **Jumbles:** BASSO PRIME JOVIAL COUPON
Answer: What the cattle tycoon made a lot of—"MOO-LA"

131. **Jumbles:** MOCHA LANKY DETACH TUMULT
Answer: What a climb up that little hill didn't do—"A-MOUNT" TO MUCH

132. **Jumbles:** BROOD TWICE GLANCE DISMAL
Answer: What the saleslady said when asked whether that new type foundation garment is really going to work—"OF CORS-ET" WILL

133. **Jumbles:** TWILL DUCHY FAMOUS APPEAR
Answer: What happened when the safety match tycoon lost his temper?—HE FLARED UP

134. **Jumbles:** EIGHT SNORT BOUGHT EXOTIC
Answer: When his tongue is loose, it's often because he is this—"TIGHT"

135. **Jumbles:** CHAMP JUMPY MUSTER BUNKER
Answer: What she does when she kisses her hockey player boyfriend—"PUCK-ERS" UP

136. **Jumbles:** MIDGE TUNED HEALTH IMPUGN
Answer: Why the flower vendor was arrested—FOR "PETAL-ING"

137. **Jumbles:** KNEEL HANDY MYSELF PIRATE
Answer: What those corduroy pillows made—HEAD LINES

138. **Jumbles:** WHOOP BORAX INJECT HAMMER
Answer: What kind of a problem did the captain face?—A "MAJOR" ONE

139. **Jumbles:** NAÏVE OUTDO FORAGE ADMIRE
Answer: What your telephone might become if you fail to pay the bill—A DEAD RINGER

140. **Jumbles:** TYPED LUNGE BUCKET ACCENT
Answer: He went to the shrink for a checkup for this—THE NECK UP

141. **Jumbles:** UNIFY OBESE GAIETY ASYLUM
Answer: Why the carpenter needed all that emergency dental work—HE BIT HIS NAILS

142. **Jumbles:** SYNOD ABHOR FORKED TACKLE
Answer: Why the employee at the car factory was fired—HE TOOK A "BRAKE"

143. **Jumbles:** VIRUS BOOTY PLAGUE AFLOAT
Answer: The baker hired—and then fired—A "LOAF-ER"

186

144. **Jumbles:** STUNG HUSKY BUNION DAINTY
Answer: When the famous star didn't show up, his stand-in became this—A STANDOUT
145. **Jumbles:** DECRY JEWEL GAINED LUNACY
Answer: That hammy magician knew how to make this disappear—THE AUDIENCE
146. **Jumbles:** BIPED MOTIF GOODLY FRUGAL
Answer: The insomniac was advised to sleep on the edge of his bed in order to do this without delay—"DROP OFF"
147. **Jumbles:** EMERY STEED MILDEW PURITY
Answer: What a belly dancer has to know how to do—TWIDDLE HER "TUM"
148. **Jumbles:** ELEGY PRIZE VASSAL FOURTH
Answer: When you invite someone to an outrageously expensive restaurant—IT SERVES YOU RIGHT
149. **Jumbles:** NOVEL FINIS ABSURD POLISH
Answer: What the guy who just pretended he was a gangster must have been—A "FALSE HOOD"
150. **Jumbles:** NERVY SWISH RITUAL STICKY
Answer: What some decided to do when trousers first became fashionable for women—SKIRT THE ISSUE
151. **Jumbles:** JERKY PUDGY WALNUT NINETY
Answer: What the sleazy restaurant that made those awful submarine sandwiches did—WENT UNDER
152. **Jumbles:** IVORY TOXIN HECKLE SALUTE
Answer: Why the judge couldn't be disturbed at dinner—HIS HONOR WAS AT "STEAK"
153. **Jumbles:** RAVEN PRIOR HUMBLE DEPICT
Answer: The barber told him stories that could do this—CURL HIS HAIR
154. **Jumbles:** MINCE UNCAP SMOKER IMPOSE
Answer: When they wanted to find out about the big bicycle merger, they interviewed this—THE "SPOKES-MAN"
155. **Jumbles:** OXIDE PROBE ENGINE DAMAGE
Answer: What the maestro called his assistant—HIS "BAND AIDE"
156. **Jumbles:** LILAC HASTY TRICKY STYMIE
Answer: What they agreed to when they organized the card game on the plane—THE SKY'S THE LIMIT
157. **Jumbles:** IRONY EXPEL PLOWED GUILTY
Answer: What happened when the price of duck feathers increased?—DOWN WENT UP
158. **Jumbles:** TITLE DITTY LIZARD TEAPOT
Answer: What the gossipy rattlesnake was—A TATTLE "TAIL"
159. **Jumbles:** IMBUE BUSHY MORTAR GULLET
Answer: Another name for a pirate ship—A "THUG" BOAT
160. **Jumbles:** FETCH LISLE WALLOP NATURE
Answer: What the prize-winning dog was—A SHOW "ARF"
161. **Jumbles:** ESTATE BEACON FEWEST TYPING HEAVEN ADDUCE
Answer: A great composer involved with surgery—AN ANESTHETIC
162. **Jumbles:** EVOLVE LOTION APIECE FIRING CARPET JOBBER
Answer: Another name for a wig—A CONVERTIBLE TOP
163. **Jumbles:** BEWARE TYPIST JAUNTY IMBIBE MIDWAY TROPHY
Answer: What a taunt might be—MORE TWIT THAN WIT
164. **Jumbles:** MARTYR SUGARY JUMPER CHORUS PHYSIC TIPTOE
Answer: What a successful boxer has to consider—THE "RIGHTS" OF OTHERS
165. **Jumbles:** CATTLE BOUNTY POLLEN ARCADE EQUATE FIERCE
Answer: When Cleopatra kept saying no, they called her this—QUEEN OF "DENIAL"

166. **Jumbles:** GOSPEL BANDIT SYMBOL USEFUL ACCORD INJECT
Answer: How some skiers have been known to jump—TO "CONTUSIONS"
167. **Jumbles:** FORMAT DECEIT VANITY MISFIT BELLOW ANYWAY
Answer: The hypocrite talks on "principles" but acts on this—"INTEREST"
168. **Jumbles:** TOUCHY BOUNCE INBORN AFFRAY DRUDGE HAIRDO
Answer: How does a monster like his potatoes?—"FRENCH-FRIGHT"
169. **Jumbles:** DOOMED BRONCO ANGINA EITHER JOYOUS IMMUNE
Answer: What all the sailors got when a ship carrying red paint collided with one carrying brown paint—"MAROONED"
170. **Jumbles:** PARDON ARMORY BROKEN EMBRYO CLAUSE GOITER
Answer: What presidential "timber" is often composed of—MOSTLY "BARK"
171. **Jumbles:** OVERDO HAMPER CARNAL MEMORY NUMBER PIGEON
Answer: What the boy scout said when he fixed the horn on the little old lady's bicycle—"BEEP REPAIRED"
172. **Jumbles:** POMADE HUNGRY GARISH ADJOIN NIBBLE CHOSEN
Answer: What they called the gangster who moved next door—THE "NEIGHBOR HOOD"
173. **Jumbles:** HUNTER FICKLE WISELY CONVOY PERMIT TEACUP
Answer: When did a dozen swimmers take the plunge?—AT THE STROKE OF TWELVE
174. **Jumbles:** PENCIL MOBILE TARGET ORATOR CHUBBY FEDORA
Answer: A cat ate cheese and waited for the mouse with this—"BAITED" BREATH
175. **Jumbles:** ANSWER FEMALE MORGUE ECZEMA PROFIT GADFLY
Answer: What they called the alligator who strolled into the hotel lobby—A "LOUNGE LIZARD"
176. **Jumbles:** EGOISM PERSON HANDLE FERVOR DISMAY SICKEN
Answer: What a man who speaks with forked tongue probably is—A SNAKE IN THE GRASS
177. **Jumbles:** OPENLY GLANCE FROLIC ANEMIA LOUNGE IMPORT
Answer: In good government, the principal men should be this—MEN OF PRINCIPLE
178. **Jumbles:** EMERGE CRAVAT BURIAL INVERT HIATUS MODERN
Answer: What kind of a conference is this, apparently?—"DISARMAMENT"
179. **Jumbles:** REDEEM POSTAL VANISH BOTANY OSSIFY TERROR
Answer: How most defeated prize-fighters leave the ring—AS "SORE" LOSERS
180. **Jumbles:** COUPLE BALLAD PACKET GAINED FORGOT TAMPER
Answer: An evening dress is sometimes designed to help the wearer catch this—A MAN - - - OR A COLD